Study Guide

Karen Moreau
Niagara College

Kimberly J. Robinson
Saint Mary's University

Arlene Lundquist
Utica College

Lisa Bauer
Utica College

The World of Psychology

Seventh Canadian Edition

Samuel E. Wood
Ellen Green Wood
Denise Boyd
Eileen Wood
Serge Desmarais

PEARSON

Toronto

Acquisitions Editor: Matthew Christian
Assistant Editor: Stephen Kass
Project Manager: Jessica Hellen
Production Editor: Raghavi Khullar, Cenveo Publisher Services
Cover Designer: Miguel Acevedo

---

10 9 8 7 6 5 4 3 2 1 WC

PEARSON

ISBN 978-0-205-93473-7

TABLE OF CONTENTS

PREFACE

HOW TO USE THIS STUDY GUIDE

Invest your time so you get the greatest benefit!

The following techniques have been shown to increase a student's mastery of new information:

- Use as many of your senses and abilities as possible—writing, reading, hearing, speaking, drawing, etc.
- Organize information so it is meaningful to you.
- Study with other people whenever possible.
- Have FUN. We remember what we enjoy.

CHAPTER OUTLINE

Class and Text Notes

This section is designed so you can take notes on these pages during lectures and also from your reading of the text. Most students find it useful to read the text and make notes before the instructor covers the material in class.

Before you begin filling out this section decide how you will tell the difference between

- your ideas
- lecture notes
- concepts from the text
- topics emphasized on the exam

The use of different colours of pens can help you differentiate each area.

Chapter Learning Objectives

After you have read and studied each chapter, you should be able to complete the learning objectives. Your exams are written based on the learning objectives so it is important to practise writing them.

Practice Multiple-Choice Test

Practice exams are an important way to check your progress. After studying the text and completing the Study Guide activities, answer these questions to determine if you need to review any areas before your exam. Answer the multiple-choice questions early enough so if you are confused about any concepts, you still have time to ask for clarification from the instructor, a tutor, or your classmates. The Pre & Post-tests and Chapter Exams on MyPsychLab are also recommended for this purpose.

Study Tips

There are study tips in the first nine chapters. These tips can help you take better notes and do better on exams. Reading all the study tips at the beginning of the semester can make your studying more effective.

Try It

The TRY IT columns apply several of your senses to the topic in the chapter. Remember, the more senses you use, the more likely it is that the information will stay with you forever.

Glossary for Text Language Enhancement

This section contains words students have identified from the text as needing more explanation. This section is for anyone who can benefit from extra support in English.

This page can be cut out, folded in half, and used as a bookmark in the appropriate chapter.

1

INTRODUCTION TO PSYCHOLOGY

CHAPTER OUTLINE

This outline provides a way to organize your notes from both the text and the lecture. It will also serve as a review for the exam.

Module 1A Introduction to Psychology	1. Psychology: Science or Common Sense? 2. The Goals of Psychology 3. What Is a Theory? 4. Basic and Applied Research

Module 1B Descriptive Research Methods	1. Naturalistic Observation: Caught in the Act of Being Themselves 2. Laboratory Observation: A More Scientific Look at the Participant 3. The Case Study Method: Studying a Few Participants in Depth 4. Survey Research: The Art of Sampling and Questioning 5. The Correlational Method: Discovering Relationships, Not Causes
Module 1C The Experimental Method: Searching for Causes	1. Independent and Dependent Variables 2. Experimental and Control Groups: The Same Except for the Treatment 3. Control in the Experiment: Attempting to Rule Out Chance 4. Generalizing the Experimental Findings: Do the Findings Apply to Other Groups? 5. Potential Problems in Experimental Research 6. Advantages and Limitations of the Experimental Method

Module 1D Participants in Psychological Research	1. Human Participants in Psychological Research 2. Psychological Tests: Assessing the Participant 3. Ethics in Research: First and Foremost 4. The Use of Animals in Research
Module 1E The Historical Progression of Psychology: Exploring the Different Perspectives	1. Wilhelm Wundt: The Founding of Psychology 2. Titchener and Structuralism: Psychology's Blind Alley 3. Functionalism: The First North American School of Psychology 4. Gestalt Psychology: The Whole Is More Than Just the Sum of Its Parts

	5. Behaviourism: Never Mind the Mind 6. Psychoanalysis: It's What's Deep Down That Counts 7. Humanistic Psychology: Looking at Human Potential 8. Cognitive Psychology: Focusing on Mental Processes
Module 1F Psychology Today	1. Current Perspectives in Psychology: Views on Behaviour and Thinking a. *Biological Perspective*: It's What's Inside That Counts b. *Evolutionary Perspective:* Adapting to the Environment c. *Sociocultural Perspective:* The Cultural Impact of Our World

2. Psychologists at Work

What are some specialties in psychology, and in what settings are they employed?

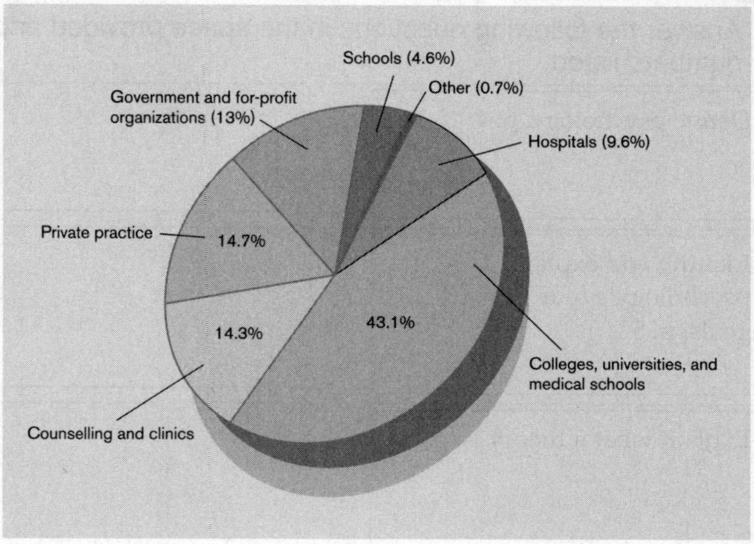

Chapter Learning Objective Questions

Answer the following questions in the space provided and check your answers on the page numbers listed.

1.1 Define psychology. p. 4	
1.2 Identify and explain psychology's four primary goals. p. 5	
1.3 Explain what a theory is. p. 5	
1.4 Compare and contrast basic and applied research. p. 6	
1.5 Identify and compare the several types of descriptive research methods. p. 6–8	
1.6 Compare and contrast naturalistic and laboratory observations, including their advantages and limitations. p. 7–8	
1.7 Compare and contrast case studies and survey research, including their advantages and shortcomings. p. 8–10	
1.8 Explain why researchers use correlational studies. p. 8	
1.9 Define what a correlation coefficient is and explain how to interpret it. p. 8	

1.10 Define the characteristics, process, advantages, and disadvantages of experimental research. p. 10–13

1.11 Define the following terms and explain their relationship to experimental research: 1) hypothesis; 2) independent and dependent variables; 3) experimental and control groups; 4) selection bias; 5) random assignment; 6) the placebo effect; 7) experimenter bias. p. 10–12

1.12 Explain why psychologists use psychological tests. p. 14

1.13 Compare and contrast reliability and validity, and explain how these two issues relate to psychological tests. p. 14

1.14 Define the following early schools of psychology: 1) structuralism; 2) functionalism; 3) Gestalt; 4) behaviourism; 5) psychoanalysis; 6) humanistic psychology; 7) cognitive psychology. p. 18–21

1.15 Describe the newer perspectives in modern psychology. p. 22–23

1.16 Compare and contrast the newer perspectives in modern psychology. p. 22–23

1.17 Identify the various fields of work available to psychologists. p. 23–24

Study Tips / Try It

Learn to study more effectively and improve your memory with these tips and practical exercises.

Improving Your Memory

1. Learn general first and then specific.
2. Make material meaningful to you.
3. Create associations with what you already know.
4. Learn it actively.
5. Imagine vivid pictures.
6. Recite aloud.
7. Reduce noise and interruptions.
8. Overlearn the material.
9. Be aware of your attitude toward information.
10. Space out learning over several days.
11. Remember related information when you are having trouble recalling something.
12. Use mnemonic devices (rhymes or words created from material).
13. Combine several of these techniques at once.

Naturalistic Observations on Campus

Try answering the following questions to experience being a researcher in naturalistic observation.

1. Go to the study areas of the library. Do you see more men or women studying there? (This may help you decide where you want to study.)
2. What is the average distance between two men walking together across campus? Does this differ for women or various ethnic groups?
3. What is the average group size of students in the cafeteria?
4. How could the information from question #3 be used by the management of the cafeteria?
5. Observe students talking. What conclusions can you make about differences among students with regard to eye contact, distance between them, and body language?

Use the SQ3R Method when studying your text

Survey

Before you read the chapter, take a visual tour of it. Notice the headings and how the material is organized. Observe tables and figures and other boxed material in the text. Read the introduction and summary statements.

Question

While you are surveying the chapter, create questions along the way. Ask yourself what questions the material appears to be addressing. If you like, write down the questions. Now you are ready to begin reading your text.

Read

Keep in mind the questions you have formulated and, as you read, seek answers to those questions. Notice bolded and italicized text, and reread complex material several times if necessary for comprehension. Divide your reading task into sections.

Recite

At the end of each reading section, recite the material. Take notes in your own words or even say it out loud. You can recite to a friend, a tape recorder, or yourself. This will help you encode the information more efficiently so it is easier to retrieve at test time.

Review

At the end of the chapter, you should go back and review all that you have learned. Develop mnemonics for anything that needs to be memorized. Use flash cards for anything that requires further practice and repetition. Go over material you found particularly difficult.

Practice Multiple-Choice Test

After studying the text and completing the Study Guide activities, answer these questions to determine if you need to review any areas before your exam.

1. Basic research is to __________ as applied research is to __________.
   a. simple; hard
   b. general knowledge; practical solutions
   c. important; frivolous
   d. scientific; intuitive

2. Naturalistic observation, the case study method, and the survey method share which of the following features?
   a. They all are descriptive research methods.
   b. None are used in physics.
   c. They each apply to limited situations.
   d. They all utilize correlation methods.

3. ______________ occurs when researchers' expectations about a situation cause them to see what they expect to see or to make incorrect inferences about the behaviour they observe.
   a. Inferential bias
   b. Experimenter bias
   c. Selection bias
   d. Situational bias

4. Psychologists use __________ to gather in-depth information about a single individual.
   a. the case study method
   b. the survey method
   c. laboratory observation
   d. naturalistic observation

5. A group of participants selected for a survey from a population are referred to as a:
   a. subpopulation.
   b. sample.
   c. subgroup.
   d. control group.

6. The total group of people to which the researchers intend to generalize their results is called the:
   a. subpopulation.
   b. control group.
   c. population.
   d. subgroup.

7. Which is an advantage of using the survey method?
   a. Large numbers of subjects can be used.
   b. Answers are usually honest and accurate.
   c. A representative sample is fairly easy to obtain.
   d. A cause-and-effect relationship can be demonstrated.

8. Which of the following research methods yields the most definite evidence of cause and effect?
   a. naturalistic observation
   b. the survey method
   c. the case study method
   d. the experimental method

9. What factor is manipulated by the researcher to determine its effect on a condition or behaviour?
   a. dependent variable
   b. independent variable
   c. control variable
   d. random variable

10. Dependent variable is to __________ as independent variable is to __________.
    a. cause; effect
    b. correlation; experiment
    c. effect; cause
    d. random; control

11. Participants are assigned to take math tests in either a warm classroom or a cold classroom. Test scores are then examined to determine whether these conditions affected performance. In this example, the independent variable is:
    a. mathematics skill.
    b. test scores.
    c. classroom temperature.
    d. not identified.

12. The __________ group of participants is exposed to the independent variable.
a. sample
b. population
c. experimental group
d. control group

13. Which of the following statements is NOT true about a control group?
a. It should be similar to an experimental group.
b. It is exposed to the independent variable.
c. At the end of the experiment, it is measured on the dependent variable.
d. It is used for purposes of comparison.

14. Participant ______________ is involved with the placebo effect.
a. hypothesis
b. idea of how other participants behave
c. experience of actual treatment
d. expectation

15. When the new drug was tested, neither the researcher nor the patients knew who was getting the new drug and who was getting a sugar pill that looked like the drug. This control was know as:
a. random assignment.
b. the self-fulfilling prophecy.
c. the single-blind technique.
d. the double-blind technique.

16. Predicting that changes in one factor are associated with changes in another can best be determined using:
a. naturalistic observation.
b. laboratory observation.
c. the case study method.
d. the correlational method.

17. Reliability refers to:
a. the ability of a test to measure what it is supposed to measure.
b. the consistency of a test.
c. how often researchers can expect a test to be right.
d. the degree of relationship of the test to another, separate factor.

18. Validity refers to:
a. the ability of a test to measure what it is supposed to measure.
b. how often researchers can expect a test to be right.
c. the consistency of a test.
d. the degree of relationship of the test to another, separate factor.

19. Which of the following correlation coefficients indicates the strongest relationship?
a. .00
b. +.40
c. +.75
d. −.76

20. Who is used most often in experiments?
a. young children in daycare settings
b. college students
c. paid adult volunteers
d. members of the lower socioeconomic class

21. Ageism occurs when clinicians:
a. treat all age groups with the same level of openness and respect.
b. make assumptions about the differences between men and women.
c. select younger clients over middle-aged clients.
d. are open to working with clients of any age group.

22. Which of the following would a behaviourist NOT consider a subject for psychological study?
a. interpersonal interactions
b. problem-solving
c. thinking
d. public speaking

23. The major emphasis of psychoanalysis is:
a. the uniqueness of human beings and their capacity for conscious choice and growth.
b. the perception of whole units or patterns.
c. the scientific study of behaviour.
d. the unconscious.

24. The ________________ perspective in psychology today focuses on how humans have evolved and adapted behaviours required for survival against various environmental pressures.
    a. biological
    b. ethological
    c. evolutionary
    d. survival

25. There are many fields of academic specializations within psychology. For example, __________ psychologists apply their knowledge of psychological research to the legal system.
    a. clinical
    b. criminal
    c. forensic
    d. organizational

Answers to Multiple-Choice Questions

Question Number	Answer	Explanation for application questions
1.	b.	Basic research seeks to acquire knowledge whereas applied research seeks resolution to particular problems.
2.	a.	Descriptive research methods summarize data gathered in non-experimental ways.
3.	b.	
4.	a.	Case histories involve the in-depth study of a person or small group of people over an extended time.
5.	b.	
6.	c.	
7.	a.	A list of questions can be given to a large number of people.
8.	d.	Only experimental methods can show cause and effect.
9.	b.	The dependent variable is the effect of the independent variable.
10.	c.	
11.	c.	The researcher manipulates the classroom temperature, so this is the independent variable.
12.	c.	The experimental group receives the treatment of the independent variable.
13.	b.	The control group does not receive the treatment.
14.	d.	
15.	d.	In a double-blind study neither the participant nor the researcher knows who has received the treatment.
16.	d.	Correlational method allows one to predict changes in two associated factors.
17.	b.	
18.	a.	
19.	d.	The closer to 1.0 (+ or –) the correlation coefficient is, the stronger the relationship.
20.	b.	College students are often used in research because they are so convenient to use.
21.	c.	
22.	c.	Behaviourists believe that research should involve observable behaviours only.
23.	d.	
24.	c.	
25.	c.	

Glossary for Text Language Enhancement

Students identified the following words from the text as needing more explanation. This page can be cut out, folded in half, and used as a bookmark for this chapter.

term	definition
phenomenon	a factor or event that can be studied
alliances	a close association among people or nations
fascination	strong attraction
imperfections	flaws or errors in something
conception	the beginning of something
thrill-seekers	people who look for exciting activities
framework	the set of main ideas in a theory
real-world	actual; practical
inferences	making a conclusion
soliciting	asking for something, e.g. help
confederate	someone who works for the researcher
sophisticated	very developed, or complex
manipulates	controls
a self-fulfilling prophecy	expected outcome occurs
arbitrarily	based on one's personal choice, may be without supporting evidence
vocational interests	occupational interests
aptitude	ability
in conjunction with	connected with
ubiquitous	seeming to be present everywhere at the same time
deterioration	break down
minimize	reduce
deficit	lower than expected level of performance
deception	the act of misleading
debriefed	told about the experiment
misconceptions	misunderstandings
profoundly	very importantly
introspection	to look inside
proponents	people supporting a certain point of view
traumatic	resulting from an emotional experience or shock
hierarchy	the structure of
interdisciplinary	bringing together different ways of studying a problem, e.g., psychology, sociology, and medicine
parallel processing	two or more things being worked on at the same time

term	definition
spurred dispositions	encouraged a person's nature or way of being

Thinking Critically

Evaluation

Consider the three major forces in psychology: behaviourism, psychoanalysis, and humanistic psychology. Which do you like most? Which do you like least? Explain.

Point/Counterpoint

This chapter discussed the issue of deception in research. Prepare convincing arguments to support each of these opinions:

a. Deception is justified in research studies.

b. Deception is not justified in research studies.

Psychology in Your Life

In this chapter you've learned something about experimental research and survey research. How will this new knowledge affect the way you evaluate research studies in articles you read or in reports you hear in the future?

2

BIOLOGY AND BEHAVIOUR

CHAPTER OUTLINE

This outline provides a way to organize your notes from both the text and the lecture. It will also serve as a review for the exam.

Module 2A The Neurons and the Neuro-transmitters	1. The Neurons: Billions of Brain Cells

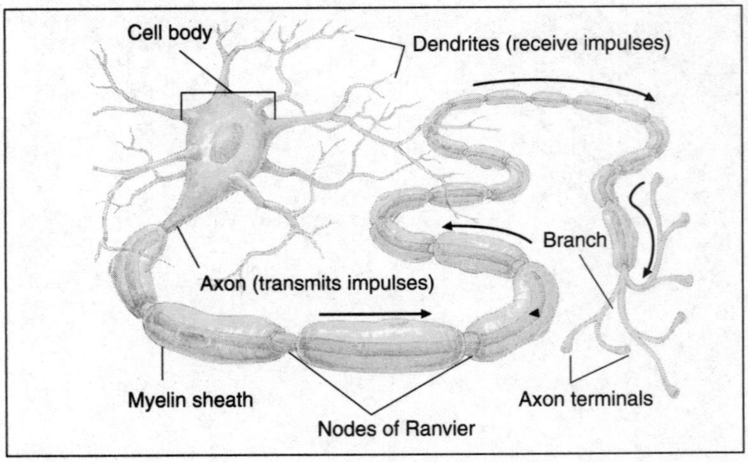

The Action Potential

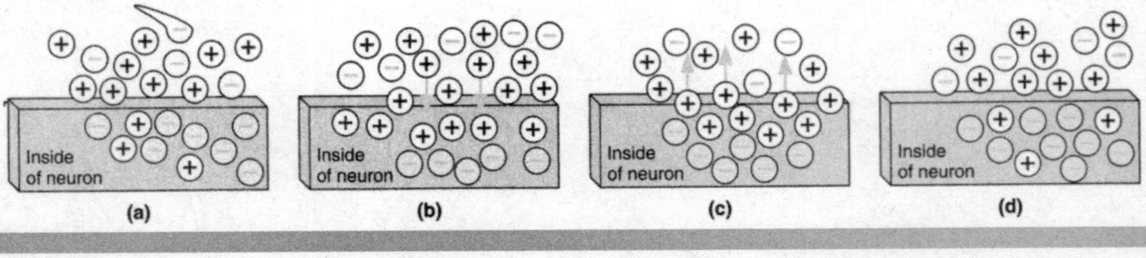

2. Neurotransmitters: The Chemical Messengers of the Brain

3. The Variety of Neurotransmitters: Some Excite and Some Inhibit

Module 2B
The Central Nervous System

1. The Spinal Cord: An Extension of the Brain

2. The Brainstem: The Most Primitive Part of the Brain

3. The Cerebellum: A Must for Graceful Movement

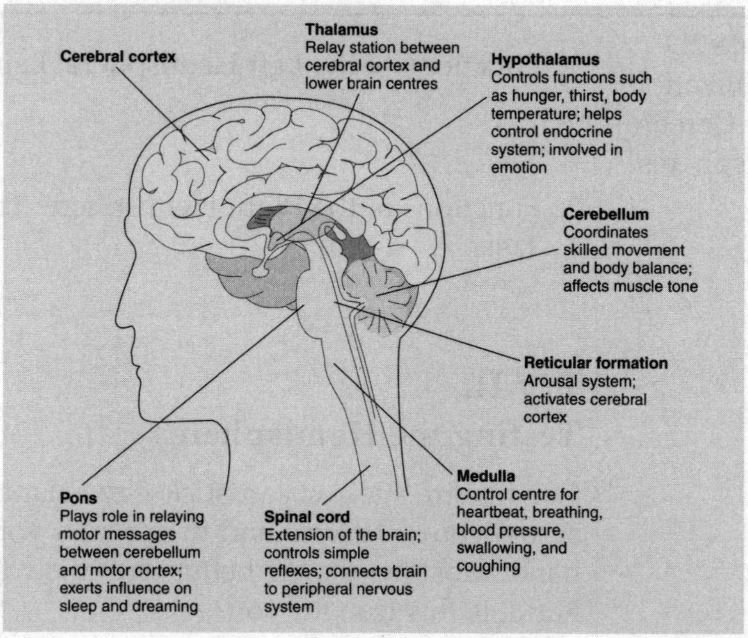

	4. The Thalamus: The Relay Station between Lower and Higher Brain Centres
	5. The Hypothalamus: A Master Regulator
	6. The Limbic System: Primitive Emotion and Memory
Module 2C The Cerebral Hemispheres	1. The Lobes of the Brain
Module 2D Specialization of the Cerebral Hemispheres	1. Functions of the Left Hemisphere: Language First and Foremost
	2. Functions of the Right Hemisphere: The Leader in Visual-Spatial Tasks

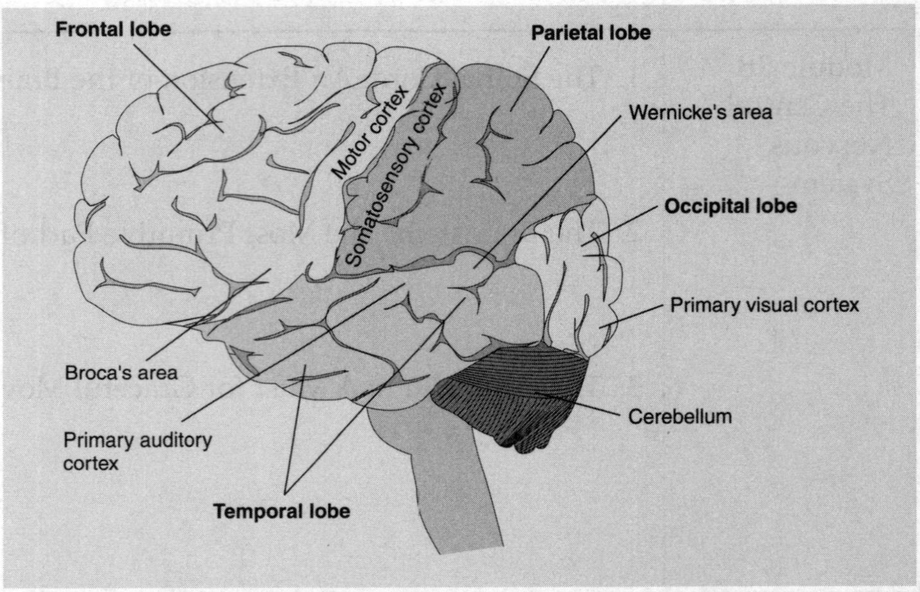

Try It!
Testing the Hemispheres

Get a metre stick or yardstick. Try balancing it across your left hand and then across your right hand. Most people are better with their dominant hand. Is this true for you?

Now try this: Begin reciting the alphabet out loud as fast as you can while balancing the stick with your left hand. Do you have less trouble this time? Why? The right hemisphere controls the act of balancing with the left hand. However, your left hemisphere, though poor at controlling the left hand, still tries to coordinate your balancing efforts. When you distract the left hemisphere with a steady stream of talk, the right hemisphere can orchestrate more efficient balancing with your left hand, without interference.

Handedness and Perception

Pick out the happy face and the sad face.

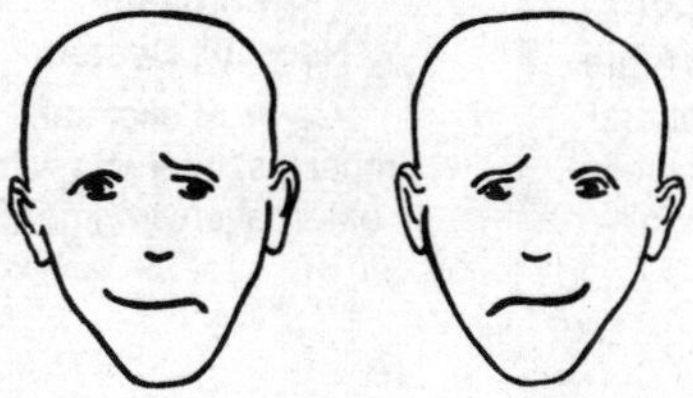

Even though the faces in the drawings are mirror images, right-handed people tend to see the face on the left as the happier face. If you are right-handed, you are likely to perceive the emotional tone revealed by the part of the face to your left as you view it (McGee & Skinner, 1987). The right hemisphere processes information from the left visual field, so right-handed people tend to be more emotionally affected by the left side of the faces they view.

3. The Split Brain: Separate Halves or Two Separate Brains?

Module 2E The Brain across the Lifespan

1. Brain Damage: Causes and Consequences

Module 2F Discovering the Brain's Mysteries

1. The EEG and the Microelectrode

2. The CT Scan and MRI

3. The PET Scan, the Functional MRI, and Other Imaging Techniques

Module 2G The Peripheral Nervous System	1. The Somatic Nervous System

The Human Nervous System

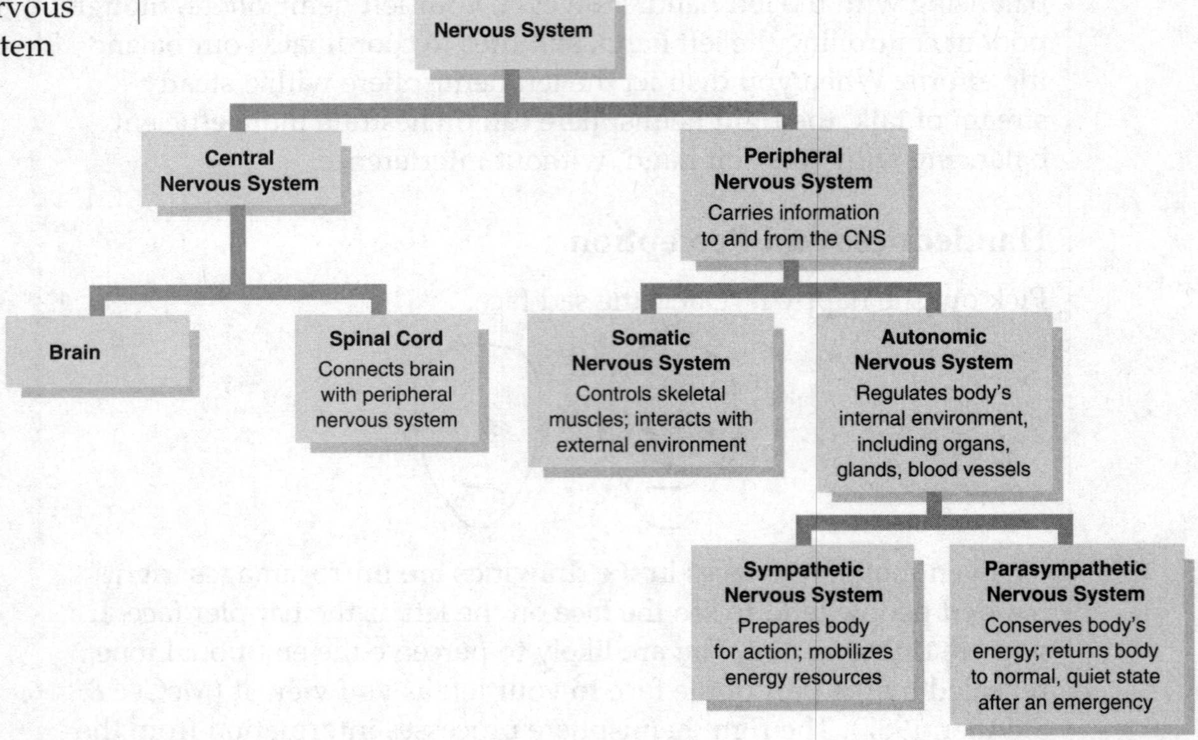

2. The Autonomic Nervous System
   - Sympathetic Nervous System
   - Parasympathetic Nervous System

Module 2H The Endocrine System	1. The Pituitary Gland 2. The Thyroid Gland 3. The Adrenal Glands 4 The Pancreas 5. The Sex Glands
Apply It!	Handedness: Does It Make a Difference?

Chapter Learning Objective Questions

Answer the following questions in the space provided and check your answers on the page numbers listed.

2.1 Define the function of the three types of neurons. p. 30–31	
2.2 Identify the three key structures of a neuron. p. 30	
2.3 Explain how neural impulses work. p. 30–32	
2.4 Contrast excitatory and inhibitory effects of neurotransmitters and how they impact on behaviour. p. 32	
2.5 Understand the role of the following neurotransmitters: acetylcholine, dopamine, norepinephrine, epinephrine, serotonin, amino acids, and endorphins. p. 33–34	
2.6 Identify the major structures of the central nervous systems: brainstem, cerebellum, thalamus, hypothalamus, and limbic system. p. 35–38	
2.7 Explain the function of each of the major structures of the central nervous system. p. 35–39	
2.8 Identify and explain the function of each of the lobes of the cerebral hemisphere. p. 40–42	

2.9 Explain how damage within a lobe might affect performance and functioning in everyday life. p. 42–43	
2.10 Contrast the functions of the left and right hemispheres. p. 44–46	
2.11 Map out the major developmental changes of the brain across the lifespan. p. 47	
2.12 Understand the impact of synaptic losses across the lifespan. p. 47	
2.13 Understand the implications that plasticity has for recovery from brain damage. p. 48	
2.14 Identify tools used to study the brain, including electroencephalograph, computerized axial tomography, magnetic resonance imaging, and positron emission tomography. p. 49–50	
2.15 Understand the kind of information that can be gained from each tool used to study the brain. p. 50	
2.16 Identify and explain the function of the two components of the peripheral nervous system. p. 51	
2.17 Explain the function of the sympathetic and parasympathetic nervous systems. p. 52	

2.18 Identify the components of the endocrine system. p. 53

2.19 Understand the role of glands and hormones within the endocrine system. p. 53–54

Study Tips

Try It

Learn to study more effectively and improve your memory with these tips and practical exercises.

Memorizing Complex Information

There are memory techniques that make learning easier and faster. One technique, known as the "loci memory system," involves picturing yourself in a familiar setting and associating it with something you need to learn. Let's assume that you needed to memorize the function and structure of a neuron. Begin by picturing yourself walking into the entry hall of your home. At the same time pretend that you are walking through a dendrite. As you walk down the hall toward the living room, imagine that you are travelling in the dendrite to the cell body. As you exit the living room and walk down the hall toward the bedrooms, think of travelling down an axon toward the terminal button that contains the neurotransmitter. In this example you are connecting new information with something very familiar. We recall information much better when we involve our imagination. An even better way to perform this exercise would be to actually walk through your home while you visualize the parts of a neuron. In this situation you would not only be using your imagination but at the same time doing something physically. It is important to realize that we have strong memories for what we do physically. Just think how long you have remembered how to ride a bike even though you may not have ridden a bike for years.

When and How to Study

1. Plan two hours of study time for every hour you spend in class.
2. Study difficult or boring subjects first.
3. Avoid long study sessions.
4. Be aware of your best time of day.
5. Use waiting time by studying flash cards.
6. Use a regular study area.
7. Don't get too comfortable.
8. Use a library.
9. Take frequent breaks.
10. Avoid noise distractions.

Hanging Onto Money

Hold a five dollar bill by the end so it's hanging down. Place the thumb and index finger of your other hand around the centre of the bill about a quarter-inch away from it. Let go of the top end with the one hand and catch the bill with the other.

This time try it with a friend. Hold the bill the same way and tell your friend to catch the bill as soon as you let it go. Most of the time your friend will not catch it. Why is this more difficult for your friend?

answer

The difference is due to the speed of the nerve impulse. When your brain sends the instruction "Let go," it also sends at the same time the instruction "Catch." Your friend's experience involves more steps: 1) see the bill being let go, 2) send a message from the eyes to the back of the brain, 3) relay message to motor area, 4) send message from motor area to muscles.

Try this on people who have had a drink or two, to see how much alcohol slows their reaction time.

Practice Multiple-Choice Test

After studying the text and completing the Study Guide activities, answer these questions to determine if you need to review any areas before your exam.

1. The __________ is a specialized cell that transmits signals throughout the nervous system.
   a. neuron
   b. myelin
   c. glial cell
   d. neurotransmitter

2. The branch-like extensions of neurons that act as the primary receivers of signals from other neurons are the:
   a. myelin sheaths.
   b. axons.
   c. cell bodies.
   d. dendrites.

3. The junction where the axon of a sending neuron communicates with a receiving neuron is called the:
   a. reuptake site.
   b . receptor site.
   c. synapse.
   d. axon terminal.

4. A reversal of the electrical potential within a neuron that happens suddenly is called:
   a. a neural discharge.
   b. a refraction.
   c. refractory impulse.
   d. an action potential.

5. The "all-or-none" law of action potentials refers to:
   a. all the neurons in a nerve fire or none of them fire.
   b. all the dendrites must be activated before a neuron fires.
   c. all the axon terminals must be in refraction or the neuron does not fire.
   d. neurons either fire at full strength or not at all.

6. When a neurotransmitter that was previously released is taken back into the axon terminal intact and ready for use again, the process is known as:
   a. reassimilation.
   b. reduction.
   c. reuptake.
   d. synaptic transfer.

7. Neurons can conduct messages faster if they have:
   a. an axon with a myelin sheath.
   b. more than one cell body.
   c. a positive resting potential charge.
   d. fewer dendrites.

8. The __________ connects the brain with the peripheral nervous system.
   a. autonomic nervous system
   b. brainstem
   c. reticular formation
   d. spinal cord

9. All of the following are controlled by the medulla EXCEPT:
   a. heart rate.
   b. arousal.
   c. breathing.
   d. blood pressure.

10. Jamie can sleep through the loud party a neighbour is having but wakes up to the phone ringing because she is expecting a call. The ______________ of her brain enables her to do this.
    a. medulla
    b. reticular formation
    c. thalamus
    d. pons

11. Which of the following regulates hunger, thirst, sexual behaviour, and many emotional experiences?
    a. thalamus
    b. amygdala
    c. hypothalamus
    d. hippocampus

12. According to the text, the part of the brain that makes us different from animals is the:

a. cerebral cortex.
b. thalamus.
c. limbic system.
d. cerebellum.

13. The two cerebral hemispheres are physically connected by a wide band of nerve fibres called the:
a. corpus callosum.
b. reticular formation.
c. amygdala.
d. nodes of Ranvier.

14. All of the following are lobes in the cerebral cortex EXCEPT the:
a. frontal lobe.
b. parietal lobe.
c. peripheral lobe.
d. temporal lobe.

15. As a consequence of damage to the right motor cortex, one might expect to have:
a. some loss of coordination on the right side of the body.
b. some loss of coordination on the left side of the body.
c. some loss of feeling on the right side of the body.
d. some loss of feeling on the left side of the body.

16. The term __________ refers to the loss or impairment of the ability to understand or communicate through writing or speaking.
a. language impairment syndrome
b. communication impairment syndrome
c. aphasia
d. agnosia

17. What area of the brain is important for planning?
a. thalamus
b. temporal lobe
c. cerebellum
d. frontal lobe

18. Which lobes of the cortex are primarily responsible for processing visual information?
a. occipital
b. parietal
c. temporal
d. frontal

19. Hearing is processed in:
a. the somatosensory cortex.
b. the primary auditory cortex.
c. Wernicke's area.
d. Broca's area.

20. For the majority of people what does their right hemisphere process?
a. speech
b. logic
c. recognition and expression of emotion
d. math

21. __________ brain waves are associated with deep relaxation.
a. Alpha
b. Beta
c. Delta
d. Theta

22. The CT scan and MRI are used to:
a. show the amount of activity in various parts of the brain.
b. measure electrical activity in the brain.
c. observe neural communication at synapses.
d. produce images of the structures within the brain.

23. Plasticity refers to:
a. the fissures of the cerebral cortex.
b. the neural condition within the axons of the cerebral hemispheres.
c. the brain's ability to reorganize and compensate for brain damage.
d. the appearance of areas of the brain that have been damaged.

24. The autonomic nervous system differs from the somatic nervous system in that its operation is largely:
a. involuntary.
b. voluntary.
c. controlled by the brain.
d. controlled by the spinal cord.

25. The pituitary gland produces hormones, which also serve as neurotransmitters, and are considered the natural opiates of the brain. These opiate-like substances are called __________.
a. acetylcholine
b. dopamine
c. norepinephrine
d. endorphins

Answers to Multiple-Choice Questions

Question Number	Answer	Explanation for application questions
1.	a.	The neuron is a specialized cell of the nervous system.
2.	d.	
3.	c.	
4.	d.	The action potential is the reversal of the electrical potential within a neuron.
5.	d.	
6.	c.	
7.	a.	Axons covered with the myelin sheath conduct the action potential more quickly than unmyelinated axons.
8.	d.	
9.	b.	The medulla controls life-sustaining, vital functions, such as heart rate, breathing, and maintaining blood pressure.
10.	b.	Our reticular formation controls selective attention and arousal.
11.	c.	
12.	a.	Our higher functions of thinking, analysis, and integrating information are processed in our cerebral cortex.
13.	a.	
14.	c.	The cerebral cortex consists of the frontal, parietal, temporal, and occipital lobes.
15.	b.	One side of the cerebral cortex controls the opposite side of the body. This is called contralateral.
16.	c.	Aphasia is a disorder of understanding language or speaking.
17.	d.	
18.	a.	
19.	b.	The primary auditory cortex processes hearing.
20.	c.	
21.	a.	
22.	d.	CT scan and MRI show structures but not function of the brain.
23.	c.	
24.	a.	
25.	d.	

Glossary for Text Language Enhancement

Students identified the following words from the text as needing more explanation. This page can be cut out, folded in half, and used as a bookmark for this chapter.

term	definition
neurosurgeons	doctors who operate on the brain
neuroradiologists	doctors who x-ray the brain
plastic surgeons	doctors who repair physical appearance
anesthetists	doctors who use drugs to make people unconscious during operations
urologists	doctors who treat problems with the urinary and genital systems
cardiologists	doctors who take care of problems with the heart
surgical nurses	nurses who specialize in operating room skills
non-functional	not working
cerebral circulation	blood flow in the brain
propagating	reproducing
remarkably	impressive
seizures	shaking of muscles
regulate	control
sprouts	divides into branches
permeable	allows fluids to enter
fuse	put together as one
intact	whole
tremors	shaking
rigidity	not flexible
metabolism	ongoing process inside the body for digesting food and getting energy from it
bombarded	to receive a lot of information very quickly
jolt	a sudden bump or shock
influential	important and having a lot of control
abruptly	suddenly
prominent	important position or role
finely coordinated	small and smooth (as in movements)
cluster	group
impairment	problem with
site	location
trajectory	the path
sustains	receives; gets
partial vision	limited vision
bursts of sound	a lot of sound heard quickly
coherent	understandable
fluent	skilful in speech

term	definition
vague	not clear
bizarre	very strange
gibberish	words that make no sense
attentional deficits	unable to focus on one thing
idiomatic	the unique style of using words for a given language
sarcastically	a statement that means the opposite of what was said and is usually negative
simultaneously	happening at the same time
amplifies	increases

Thinking Critically

Evaluation

Using your knowledge about how the human brain has been studied in the past and today, point out the advantages and the disadvantages of the older investigative methods: the case study, the autopsy, and the study of people with brain injuries or who have had brain surgery (including the split-brain operation). Follow the same procedure to discuss the more modern techniques: EEG, CT scan, PET scan, and fMRI.

Point/Counterpoint

A continuing controversial issue is whether animals should be used in biopsychological research. Review the chapter and find each occasion in which animals were used to advance our knowledge of the brain. Using what you have read in this chapter and any other information you have acquired, prepare arguments to support each of the following positions:

a. The use of animals in research projects is ethical and justifiable because of the possible benefits to humankind.
b. The use of animals in research projects is not ethical or justifiable on the grounds of possible benefits to humankind.

Psychology in Your Life

How would your life change if you had a massive stroke in your left hemisphere? How would it change if the stroke were in your right hemisphere? Which stroke would be more tragic for you, and why?

3

SENSATION AND PERCEPTION

CHAPTER OUTLINE

This outline provides a way to organize your notes from both the text and the lecture. It will also serve as a review for the exam.

Module 3A Sensation: The Sensory World	
	1. The Absolute and Difference Thresholds: To Sense or Not to Sense
	2. Signal Detection Theory
	3. Transduction and Adaptation: Transforming Sensory Stimuli into Neural Impulses

Module 3B Vision	1. Light: What We See 2. The Eye: Window to the Visual Sensory World 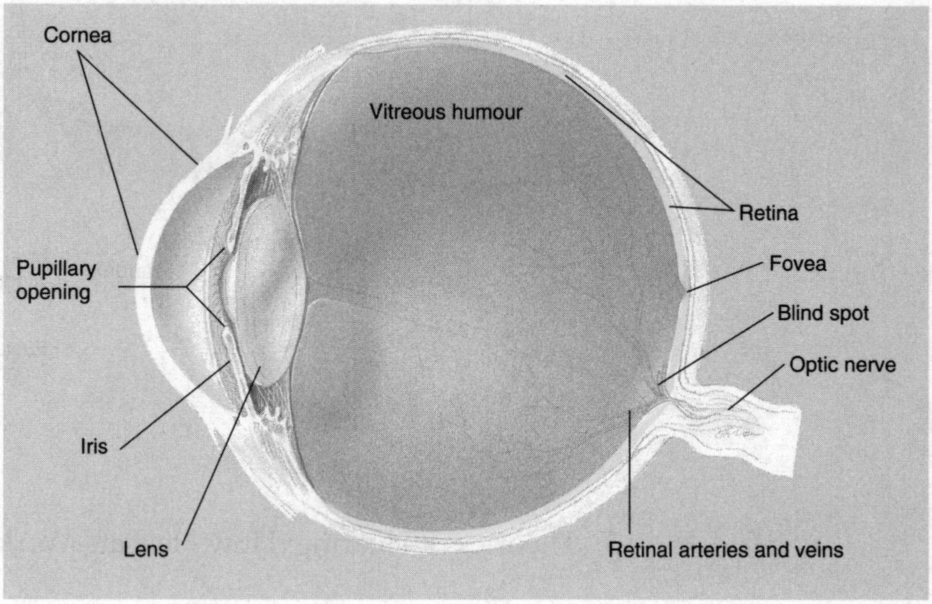 3. Colour Vision: A Multicoloured World
Module 3C Hearing	1. Sound: What We Hear 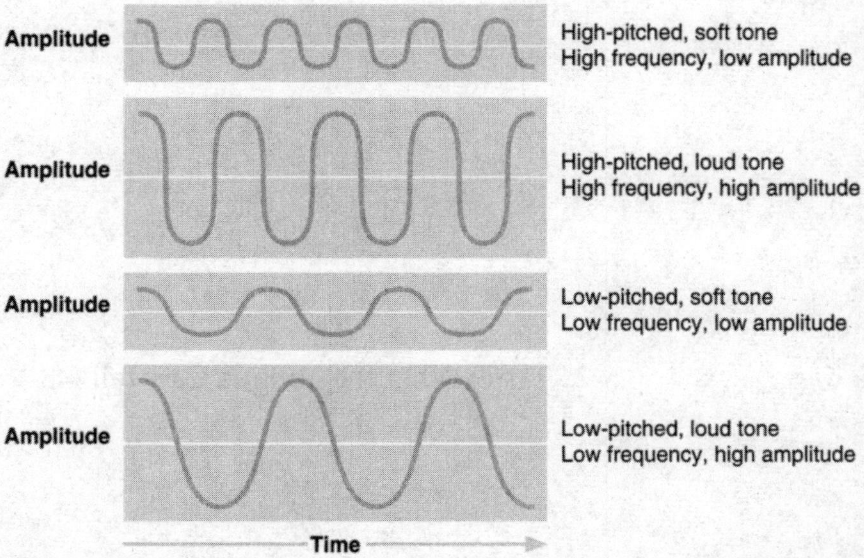

2. The Ear: More to It Than Meets the Eye

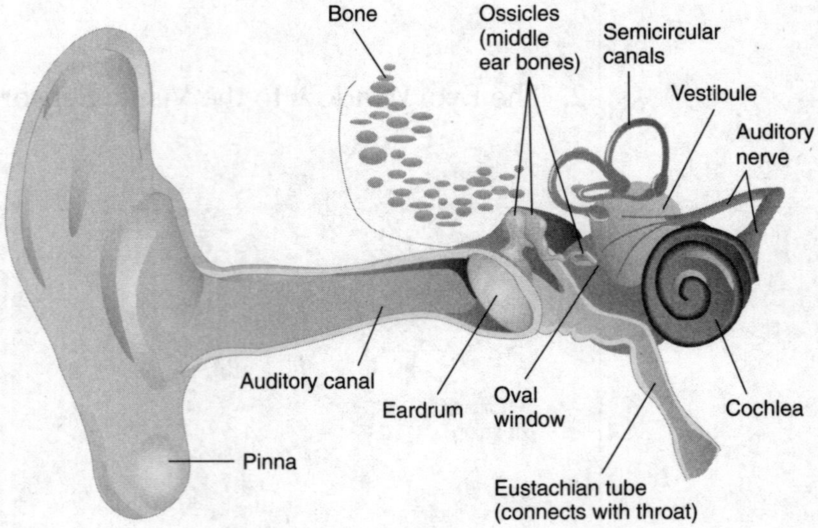

3. Theories of Hearing: How Hearing Works

4. Hearing Loss: Kinds and Causes

Module 3D Smell and Taste

1. Smell: Sensing Scents

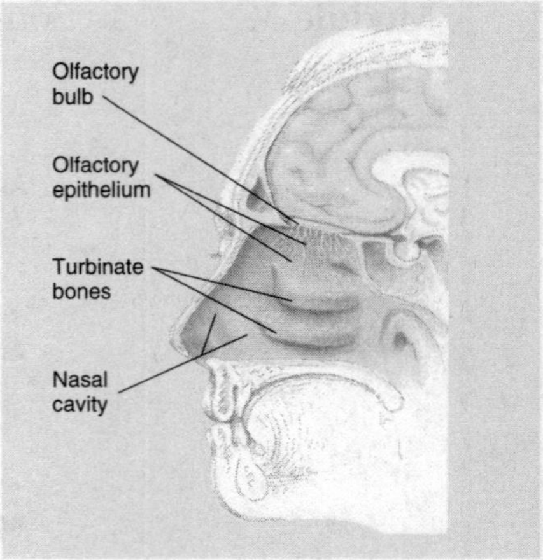

2. Taste: What the Tongue Can Tell

Module 3E The Skin Senses: Information from Our Natural Clothing

1. The Mechanism of Touch: How Touch Works

2. Pain: Physical Hurts

Module 3F The Spatial Orientation Senses

1. The Kinesthetic Sense: Keeping Track of Our Body Parts

2. The Vestibular Sense: Sensing Up and Down and Changes in Speed

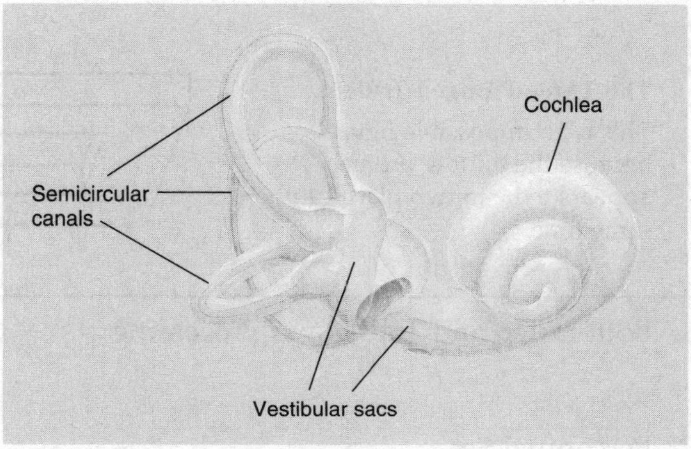

Module 3G Perception: Ways of Perceiving

Reversing Figure and Ground

1. The Gestalt Principles of Perceptual Organization

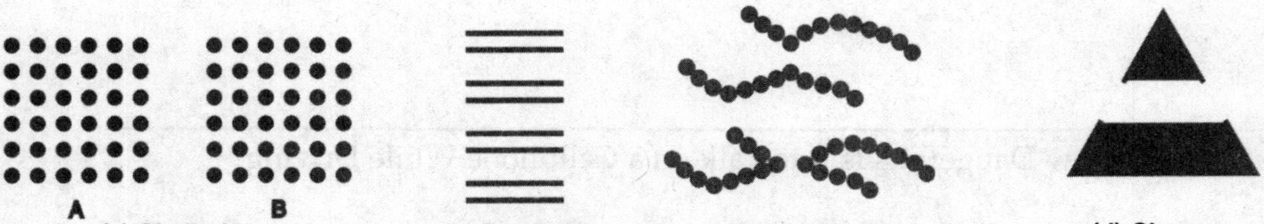

(a) Similarity (b) Proximity (c) Continuity (d) Closure

	2. Perceptual Constancy 3. Depth Perception: What's Up Close and What's Far Away 4. Ambiguous Figures: More Than One Way to See Them **The Three-Pronged Trident** This is an impossible figure because the middle prong appears to be in two places at the same time. 
Module 3H Additional Influences on Perception	1. Bottom-Up and Top-Down Processing 2. Perceptual Set 3. Attention
Apply It!	How Dangerous Is It to Talk on a Cellphone While Driving?

Chapter Learning Objective Questions

Answer the following questions in the space provided and check your answers on the page numbers listed.

3.1 Identify and understand the difference between sensation and perception. p. 62

3.2 Define and explain each of the following measures of the senses: absolute threshold, difference threshold, and signal detection theory. p. 62–63

3.3 Understand how sensory stimuli come to be experienced as sensations. p. 63

3.4 Identify and describe the major structures of the eye. p. 65–66

3.5 Compare the function of rods and cones. p. 66

3.6 Define and compare the two theories of colour vision. p. 68–69

3.7 Explain the relative contributions of the two theories of colour vision. p. 69

3.8 Define colour blindness. p. 70

3.9 Identify and define the major structures used for hearing. p. 73

3.10 Compare and contrast the two theories of hearing. p. 73–74

3.11 Define olfaction and gustation. p. 75–76	
3.12 Identify the structures and the role of the structures used for smell and taste. p. 75–76	
3.13 Explain how the skin provides sensory information. p. 77	
3.14 Explain the gate-control theory. p. 78	
3.15 Explain the role of endorphins. p. 78–79	
3.16 Identify the kinds of information provided by the kinesthetic sense. p. 79	
3.17 Describe the vestibular sense. p. 81	
3.18 Identify and explain the four Gestalt principles of grouping. p. 82	
3.19 Identify the four types of constancies. p. 82–83	
3.20 Define binocular depth cues. p. 84	

3.21 Identify and give an example of the seven monocular depth cues. p. 84

3.22 Compare and contrast top-down and bottom-up processing. p. 85

Study Tips | Try It

Learn to study more effectively and improve your memory with these tips and practical exercises.

Study in Groups

Research has shown that one of the most effective ways to learn is to study with other students. Your grades on exams will be better and you will have a lot more fun doing it!

How to Form a Group

1. Look for dedicated students who share some of your academic goals and challenges.
2. You could write a note on the blackboard asking interested students to contact you, or pass around a sign-up sheet before class.
3. Limit groups to five or six people.
4. Test the group by planning a one-time-only session. If that session works, plan another.

Possible Activities for a Study Group

1. Compare notes.
2. Have discussions and debates about the material.
3. Test each other with questions brought to the group meeting by each member.
4. Practise teaching each other.
5. Brainstorm possible test questions.
6. Share suggestions for problems in the areas of finances, transportation, child care, time scheduling, or other barriers.
7. Develop a plan at the beginning of each meeting from the list above or any ideas you have.

What Do You Perceive?

Do these steps go on continuously?

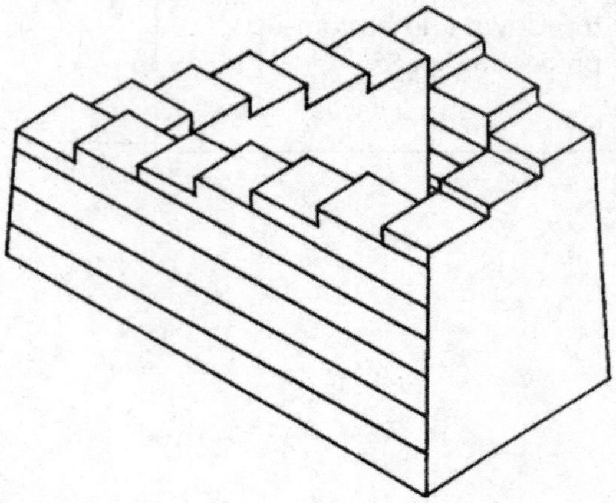

In the figure below, which long lines are parallel?

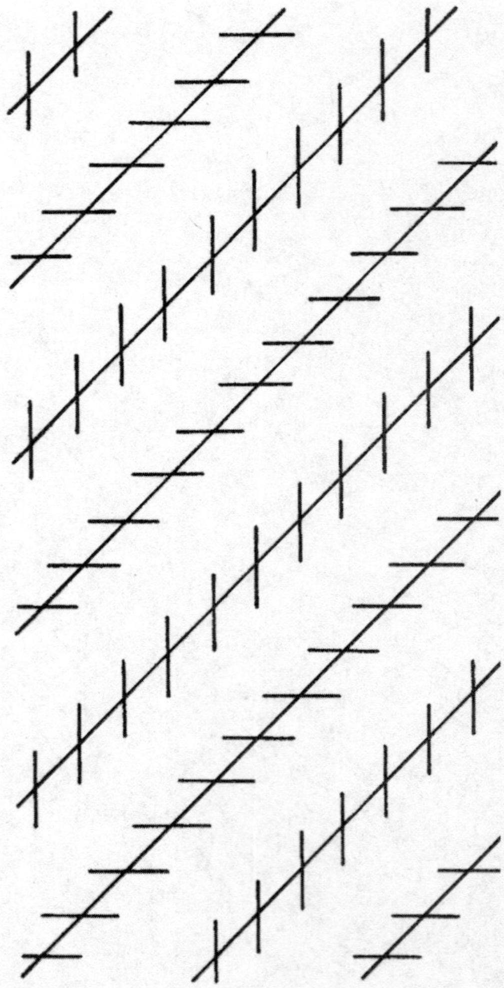

Practice Multiple-Choice Test

After studying the text and completing the Study Guide activities, answer these questions to determine if you need to review any areas before your exam.

1. The detection of sensory stimuli and transmission back to the brain is called:
   a. sensation.
   b. reception.
   c. consciousness.
   d. perception.

2. The __________ process involves interpretation and organization of information brought to us by our various senses.
   a. somnambulism
   b. sensation
   c. perception
   d. convergence

3. Absolute threshold is the minimum amount of sensory stimulation that a person can:
   a. never detect.
   b. always detect.
   c. detect in at least one in ten trials.
   d. detect 50 percent of the time.

4. The __________ process involves sensory receptors converting sensory stimulation into neural impulses.
   a. sublimation
   b. transduction
   c. convergence
   d. refraction

5. Light moves toward the retina in which of the following paths?
   a. lens, cornea, pupil
   b. pupil, lens, cornea
   c. pupil, cornea, lens
   d. cornea, pupil, lens

6. Our pupils do not dilate:
   a. when telling a lie.
   b. in bright light.
   c. while becoming angry.
   d. when we are sexually aroused.

7. All of the following are true of cones EXCEPT:
   a. They play a key role in colour vision.
   b. They are critical in our ability to notice fine detail.
   c. They function best in bright light.
   d. They are more numerous than rods.

8. Which of the following sets of colours are the three types of cones particularly sensitive to?
   a. yellow, red, and blue
   b. red, white, and blue
   c. green, blue, and yellow
   d. red, green, and blue

9. After leaving each eye, the optic nerves come together at a point:
   a. where the information is interpreted by the brain.
   b. where information from each eye is combined into one impulse.
   c. deep in the pons.
   d. where some of the nerve fibres cross to the opposite side of the brain.

10. Saturation refers to the:
    a. intensity of the colour we view.
    b. brightness of the colour we view.
    c. purity of the colour we view.
    d. wavelength of the colour we view.

11. Which of the following statements is NOT true of the amplitude of sound?
    a. It is measured in decibels.
    b. It is mainly the pitch of the sound.
    c. It depends on the magnitude of a sound wave.
    d. It depends on the energy of a sound wave.

12. Which of the following is not a name of one of the bones in the middle ear?
    a. mallet
    b. anvil
    c. hammer
    d. stirrup

13. The hair cells are contained:
   a. within the auditory nerve.
   b. along the inner membrane of the eardrum.
   c. in the tiny bones of the inner ear.
   d. within the cochlea.

14. When you listen to a recording of your own voice, what is the main reason that it sounds so odd to you?
   a. You typically do not pay attention to your own voice.
   b. You are being too self-conscious.
   c. You are hearing it without bone conduction.
   d. Recording equipment greatly distorts the human voice.

15. Place theory and frequency theory are two explanations of:
   a. colour blindness.
   b. sound localization.
   c. auditory threshold shift.
   d. pitch perception.

16. Conductive hearing loss can be caused by:
   a. injury to the eardrum or ossicles.
   b. injury to the hair cells and auditory nerve.
   c. injury to the auditory nerve or semicircular canals.
   d. injury to the semicircular canals and the ossicles.

17. ____________ probably plays the biggest role in nerve deafness.
   a. Lifelong exposure to excessive noise
   b. Disease
   c. Birth defects
   d. Aging

18. Hearing aids are not useful if the damage is to the:
   a. cochlea.
   b. anvil.
   c. pistole.
   d. auditory nerve.

19. The largest sense organ is sensitive to:
   a. chemical concentration.
   b. touch.
   c. sound.
   d. light.

20. The ____________ theory suggests that nerve fibres carrying messages that pressure is being applied to some part of the body can prevent messages from getting through to the brain.
   a. gate-control theory
   b. opponent-process theory
   c. volley principle
   d. Gestalt principle

21. What causes "runner's high"?
   a. naloxone
   b. endorphins
   c. placebo
   d. epinephrine

22. Information about the position of body parts and about body movement, detected by receptors in the muscles, ligaments, and joints, is referred to as:
   a. the vestibular sense.
   b. the gustatory sense.
   c. the tactile sense.
   d. the kinesthetic sense.

23. The vestibular sense:
   a. integrates sensations from the chemical senses.
   b. monitors the internal organs of the body.
   c. provides information about the position of body parts.
   d. provides information about movement and our orientation in space.

24. The most fundamental principle of perceptual organization is called the:
   a. figure-ground relationship.
   b. volley principle.
   c. monocular phenomenon.
   d. law of closure.

25. The tendency to perceive objects as maintaining the same size, shape, and brightness despite differences in distance, viewing angle, and lighting is called perceptual:
   a. organization.
   b. rigidity.
   c. adaptation.
   d. constancy.

Answers to Multiple-Choice Questions

Question Number	Answer	Explanation for application questions
1.	a.	Sensation is the process of "taking in" sensory information.
2.	c.	Perception is the process of "interpreting" sensory information.
3.	d.	
4.	b.	
5.	d.	Light goes through the cornea and the pupil, and then strikes the retina.
6.	b.	Our pupil constricts in bright light to protect the eye from damage.
7.	d.	There are many more rods than cones.
8.	d.	
9.	a.	
10.	c.	
11.	b.	
12.	a.	The middle ear's bones are the anvil, hammer, and stirrup.
13.	d.	Hair cells are on the basilar membrane in the cochlea.
14.	c.	
15.	d.	
16.	a.	Conductive hearing loss may be caused by loud noise.
17.	a	
18.	d.	
19.	b.	Skin is our largest sense organ.
20.	a.	
21.	b.	Endorphins are chemicals made in the brain that result in pain reduction and a feeling of euphoria.
22.	d.	
23.	d.	
24.	a.	
25.	d.	

Glossary for Text Language Enhancement

Students identified the following words from the text as needing more explanation. This page can be cut out, folded in half, and used as a bookmark for this chapter.

term	definition
transmit	send
rudimentary	simple; not fully developed
fundamental	basic element or part
scant	little or few
dimmest	lowest
arbitrarily	based on one's preference
vintage	a particular type, or year
scan a sea of faces	look at many people's faces
diminish	reduce
circular	round
subtle	hardly noticeable
dilate	open up to be larger
suspended	hanging
composed of	made up of
transparent	able to see through
correctable	can be fixed
decreases sharply	decreases quickly
encode	change into
occupied	filled
adapt	make changes
absorbed	taken in
defects	problems
dispel	to drive away
distinguish	to tell the difference between
pulsating	to beat or throb
flute	a musical instrument in which air is blown into the mouthpiece
oddly shaped	not the usual shape
synchronized	working together
endure	having to put up with something, usually not nice
noxious fumes	harmful gas
inhalant	used to breathe in medicine
cluster	group together
crevice	a narrow crack or split
depresses the skin	pushes in on the skin
persists	continues
coursing	flowing
literal	using the most common meaning of the word
converge	come together

term	definition
ambiguous overhead to decipher	not clear meaning above us to figure out; understand

Thinking Critically

Evaluation

Using what you have learned about the factors that contribute to hearing loss, prepare a statement indicating what the government should do to control noise pollution, even to the extent of banning certain noise hazards. Consider the workplace, the home, toys, machinery, rock concerts, and so on.

Point/Counterpoint

Much commercial advertising is aimed at providing products that reduce or eliminate pain. Prepare a sound, logical argument supporting one of the following positions:

a. Pain is valuable and necessary.
b. Pain is not necessary.

Psychology in Your Life

Vision and hearing are generally believed to be the two most highly prized senses. How would your life change if you lost your sight? How would your life change if you lost your hearing? Which sense would you find more traumatic to lose? Why?

4

STATES OF CONSCIOUSNESS

CHAPTER OUTLINE

This outline provides a way to organize your notes from both the text and the lecture. It will also serve as a review for the exam.

Module 4A Circadian Rhythms: Our 24-Hour Highs and Lows	1. The Suprachiasmatic Nucleus: The Body's Timekeeper 2. Jet Lag: Where Am I and What Time Is It? 3. Shift Work: Working Day and Night

Module 4B Sleep: That Mysterious One-Third of Our Lives	1. NREM and REM Sleep: Watching the Eyes 2. Sleep Cycles: The Nightly Pattern of Sleep 3. Individual Differences in Sleep Patterns: How We Differ 4. REM Sleep: A Part of Sleep That We Should Not Do Without 5. Dreaming: Mysterious Mental Activity While We Sleep
Module 4C Variations in Sleep and Sleep Disorders	1. Variations in Sleep 2. Parasomnias: Unusual Behaviours During Sleep 3. Major Sleep Disorders

Brain-Wave Patterns Associated with Different Stages of Sleep

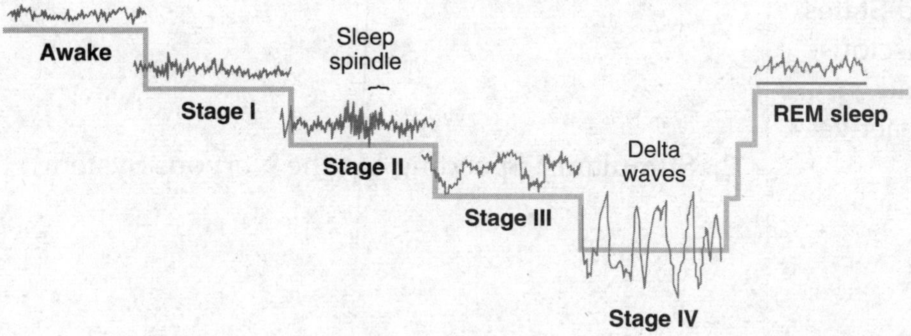

Module 4D Altering Consciousness through Concentration and Suggestion	1. Meditation: Expanded Consciousness or Relaxation? 2. Hypnosis: Look into My Eyes
Module 4E Altered States of Consciousness and Psychoactive Drugs	1. Drug Dependence: Slave to a Substance 2. Stimulants: Speeding Up the Nervous System 3. Hallucinogens: Seeing, Hearing, and Feeling What Is Not There 4. Depressants: Slowing Down the Nervous System 5. How Drugs Affect the Brain
Apply It!	• How to Get a Good Night's Sleep

Chapter Learning Objective Questions

Answer the following questions in the space provided and check your answers on the page numbers listed.

4.1 Define circadian rhythms and explain how they influence sleep. p. 98	
4.2 Explain the importance of the suprachiasmatic nucleus. p. 98–99	
4.3 Describe the problems associated with shift work. p. 99	
4.4 Define and compare NREM and REM sleep. p. 101	
4.5 Describe the pattern of sleep cycles. p. 102–103	
4.6 Explain how age influences sleep. p. 103	
4.7 Define larks and owls and describe their different sleep patterns. p. 103	
4.8 Describe the function of sleep and how sleep deprivation affects functioning. p. 104	
4.9 Compare REM and NREM dreams. p. 104	
4.10 Describe the factors that influence how much sleep we need. p. 107	

4.11 Define parasomnia. p. 107

4.12 Describe and compare the different types of parasomnia. p. 107–108

4.13 Describe and compare the different types of major sleep disorder. p. 108–109

4.14 Define meditation and describe its purpose. p. 110

4.15 Define hypnosis and describe its use. p. 110–111

4.16 Define psychoactive drugs. p. 112

4.17 Describe and contrast drug dependence and drug tolerance. p. 112–125

4.18 Explain what factors influence the addictive potential of a drug. p. 113

4.19 Identify the most common types of stimulants and describe their effects. p. 113–114

4.20 Identify the most common types of hallucinogens and describe their effects. p. 114–115

4.21 Describe the effects of marijuana. p. 115–116

4.22 Identify the three most common types of depressants and describe their effects. p. 116–117

Study Tips | Try It

Learn to study more effectively and improve your memory with these tips and practical exercises.

Better Test Taking

1. Predict the test questions. Ask your instructor to describe the test format—how long it will be, and what kind of questions to expect (essay, multiple choice, problems, etc.).
2. Have a section in your notebook labelled "Test Questions" and add several questions to this section after every lecture and after reading the text. Record topics instructors repeat several times or go back to in subsequent lectures. Write down questions the instructor poses to students.
3. Arrive early so you can do a relaxation exercise. (There's one in Chapter 4 of our textbook.)
4. Ask about the procedure for asking questions during the test.
5. Know the rules for taking the test so you do not create the impression of cheating.
6. Scan the whole test immediately. Budget your time based on how many points each section is worth.
7. Read the directions slowly. Then reread them.
8. Answer the easiest, shortest questions first. This gives you the experience of success and stimulates associations. This prepares your mind for more difficult questions.
9. Next, answer multiple-choice, true-false, and fill-in-the-blank questions.
10. Use memory techniques when you're stuck.
    - If your recall on something is blocked, remember something else that's related.
    - Start from the general and go to the specific.
11. Look for answers in other test questions. A term, name, date, or other fact that you can't remember might appear in the test itself.
12. Don't change an answer unless you are sure because your first instinct is usually best.

(See Study Tips Chapter 5 for more test-taking hints.)

Relaxing through Meditation

Find a quiet place and sit in a comfortable position.

1. Close your eyes.
2. Relax all your muscles deeply. Begin with your feet and move slowly upward, relaxing the muscles in your legs, buttocks, abdomen, chest, shoulders, neck, and finally your face. Allow your whole body to remain in this deeply relaxed state.
3. Now concentrate on your breathing, and breathe in and out through your nose. Each time you breathe out, silently say the word om to yourself.
4. Repeat this process for 20 minutes. (You can open your eyes to look at your watch periodically, but don't use an alarm.) When you are finished, remain seated for a few minutes—first with your eyes closed, and then with them open.

Benson recommends that you maintain a passive attitude. Don't try to force yourself to relax. Just let it happen. If a distracting thought comes to mind, ignore it and just repeat om each time you exhale. It is best to practise this exercise once or twice each day, but not within two hours of your last meal. Digestion interferes with the relaxation response.

How to Get a Good Night's Sleep

How would you describe your own sleep habits? Could they stand a bit of improvement? To assist you is getting enough sleep, here is a list of tips compiled by researchers at the Mayo Clinic (2006). Here are a few highlights:

- Keep a regular schedule that includes fairly consistent times for going to bed and getting up.
- Avoid eating or drinking to excess just before going to bed.
- Limit your intake of nicotine and caffeine throughout the day.

- Get regular exercise.
- Maintain a comfortable temperature and light level in the place where you sleep.
- Do not nap during the day.
- Make your bed as comfortable as possible.
- Establish a going-to-bed routine that relaxes you.
- Do not lie in bed awake for more than 30 minutes. Get up and do something until you feel sleepy enough to go back to bed.
- Don't push yourself to stay awake beyond the point at which you begin to feel sleepy.
- Avoid resorting to sleep medications unless absolutely necessary.

Using Your Dreams

History is full of cases where dreams have been a pathway to creativity and discovery. Otto Loewi, a pharmacologist, had spent years studying the chemical transmission of nerve impulses. A tremendous breakthrough in his research came when he dreamed of an experiment three nights in a row. The first two nights he woke up and scribbled the experiment on paper. But the next morning, he couldn't tell what the notes meant. On the third night, he got up after having the dream. This time, instead of making notes he went straight to his laboratory and performed the experiment. Loewi later said that if the experiment had occurred to him while awake he would have rejected it, but instead he won the Nobel Prize!

Being able to take advantage of dreams for problem solving is improved if you think intently about a problem before you go to bed. State the problem clearly and review all important information.

How to Remember Your Dreams

1. Keep a pen and paper or tape recorder beside your bed and plan to remember your dreams.
2. If possible try to awaken gradually without an alarm. Natural awakening is almost always soon after a REM period.
3. If you rarely remember your dreams, you may want to set an alarm clock for one hour before you usually get up. Although not as effective as waking up naturally, this method may help you remember a dream.
4. When you wake up, lie still and review the dream images with your eyes closed. Try to recall as many details as possible.
5. If you can, make your first dream notes (written or taped) with your eyes still closed. Describe feelings, plot, characters, and actions of the dream.
6. Review the dream again and record as many additional details as you can remember. Dream memories disappear quickly.
7. Keep a diary and review it periodically, which will reveal recurrent themes, conflicts, and emotions. This often produces insights.

Practice Multiple-Choice Test

After studying the text and completing the Study Guide activities, answer these questions to determine if you need to review any areas before your exam.

1. During REM sleep, brain activity _________ while body movements _________.
   a. decreases; increase
   b. increases; decrease
   c. increases; are the same as in NREM sleep
   d. is the same as in NREM sleep; decrease

2. ___________ dreams have a narrative or dreamlike quality and are more visual, vivid, emotional, and peculiar than ___________ dreams, which characteristically are cognitive (i.e., resembling thought).
   a. NREM; ordinary
   b. lucid; REM
   c. REM; NREM
   d. symbolic; telepathic

3. Circadian rhythms are the regular fluctuations from high to low points of certain bodily functions that occur over the course of:
   a. a day.
   b. an hour.
   c. a week.
   d. a month or longer.

4. The internal biological clock seems to operate on a __________ hour day when external cues are eliminated.
   a. 21
   b. 23
   c. 25
   d. 27

5. The main reason for jet lag is that:
   a. travellers lose a night's sleep.
   b. the traveller's internal biological clock is no longer synchronized with clock time.
   c. airline travel disrupts body temperature.
   d. jet travel temporarily disrupts the suprachiasmatic nucleus.

6. Which of the following is NOT characteristic of people who work rotating shifts?
   a. disturbed sleep
   b. digestive problems
   c. greater efficiency and alertness during subjective night
   d. increased tendency to use caffeine, alcohol, and sleeping pills

7. Research suggests that rotating work schedules from days to evenings to nights and changing work schedules every three weeks rather than every week results in:
   a. more health problems.
   b. no change in worker productivity.
   c. high personnel turnover.
   d. higher work satisfaction.

8. Which of the following is NOT characteristic of REM sleep?
   a. paralysis of large muscles
   b. dreaming
   c. delta waves
   d. increase in blood pressure, heart rate, and respiration

9. The average length of a sleep cycle in adults is:
   a. 30 minutes.
   b. 60 minutes.
   c. 90 minutes.
   d. 120 minutes.

10. How many sleep cycles does the average person have each night?
    a. one
    b. three
    c. five
    d. seven

11. Bruce will be 75 years old in several months. Which of the following would be true of his sleep if he is typical of aging adults?
    a. He will have more awakenings and less deep sleep.
    b. He will have deeper sleep with fewer dreams.
    c. He will sleep longer than he did when he was 40.
    d. He will be more able to sleep anywhere.

12. Which age group is usually sleepy during the day regardless of the amount of sleep at night?
    a. infants
    b. children from age six to puberty
    c. adolescents
    d. the elderly

13. When comparing larks to owls:
    a. owls have a higher overall level of activation.
    b. owls and larks are subjective categories and cannot be distinguished by biological patterns.
    c. owls have a peak in body temperature earlier than do larks.
    d. larks have higher body temperatures in the morning but lower temperatures in the evening than do owls.

14. According to the text, most North Americans get:
    a. too little sleep.
    b. just the right amount of sleep.
    c. too much sleep.
    d. too little sleep in childhood and too much as adults.

15. Psychologists believe that REM sleep serves a role in all of the following EXCEPT:
    a. learning complex skills.
    b. growing new neurons.
    c. erasing trivial memories.
    d. forming permanent memories.

16. Which of the following is a sleep disturbance during which a child partially awakens from Stage 4 sleep with a scream, is dazed, and in a panic state?
    a. sleep apnea
    b. somnambulism
    c. night terror
    d. narcolepsy

17. People who fall asleep suddenly at inappropriate times may have a sleep disorder called:
    a. narcolepsy.
    b. sleep apnea.
    c. social rudeness.
    d. somnambulism.

18. Which sleep disorder involves loud snoring and the cessation (stopping) of breathing during sleep?
    a. sleep apnea
    b. insomnia
    c. narcolepsy
    d. enuresis

19. Taking sleeping pills or a few drinks before bedtime usually results in all of the following EXCEPT:
    a. lighter sleep.
    b. less sleep overall.
    c. delayed sleep onset.
    d. more awakenings during the night.

20. Which of the following is a form of contemplation used to increase relaxation, block out worries and distractions, or foster a different form of consciousness?
    a. hypnosis
    b. cognitive withdrawal
    c. hypermnesia
    d. meditation

21. Hypnosis has proven most useful in treating:
    a. obesity.
    b. pain.
    c. drug abuse.
    d. alcoholism.

22. Which of the following is true regarding psychological dependence on drugs?
    a. It is easier to combat than physical addiction.
    b. It is harder to overcome than physical addiction.
    c. It is as difficult to overcome as physical addiction.
    d. There is no such thing.

23. Which part of our brain acts as our biological clock?
    a. circadian lobe
    b. thalamus
    c. pons
    d. suprachiasmatic nucleus

24. The average number of hours people sleep during the week is _______.
    a. 7.5
    b. 6.5
    c. 9
    d. 6

25. Recent research has shown that ________ may have a range of positive health effects, including lowering blood pressure, cholesterol levels, and other measures of cardiovascular risk.
    a. meditation
    b. hypnosis
    c. nightmares
    d. MDMA

Answers to Multiple-Choice Questions

Question Number	Answer	Explanation for application questions
1.	b.	
2.	c.	
3.	a.	Circadian rhythms fluctuate in regular patterns in a 24-hour period.
4.	c.	
5.	b.	
6.	c.	
7.	d.	
8.	c.	
9.	c.	
10.	c.	
11.	a.	
12.	c.	
13.	d.	
14.	a.	
15.	b.	
16.	c.	
17.	a.	
18.	a.	
19.	c.	
20.	d.	
21.	b.	
22.	b.	
23.	d.	
24.	a.	
25.	a.	

Glossary for Text Language Enhancement

Students identified the following words from the text as needing more explanation. This page can be cut out, folded in half, and used as a bookmark for this chapter.

term	definition
ramifications	the result of somthing
advocacy	act of defending someone
adage	an old saying
imprecise	not accurate
fluctuation	increases and decreases
disrupted	interfered with
abruptly	suddenly, quickly
synchronized	occur at the same time
restorative	to bring back to the original condition
darting	moving quickly
erection	penis elongated
substantial	real; strong or solid
fumble	reach for in a clumsy way
snooze button	button to push on alarm that gives you 5 minutes more sleep
stupor	lack of alertness
larks	birds that like early morning hours
party pooper	person who is not fun at parties
contrary	opposite
lapses	gaps and problems
nodding	starting to sleep
rebound	increased amount to make up for loss
consolidation	combining together
bizarre	weird, odd
recurring	happening again and again
gasp	try to breathe hard
jet lag	sleep problems due to flying to a different time zone
trance-like	daze or daydream-like
misconceptions	not understand
violate	break
cope with	deal with
thrill	excitement
craving	desire
urge	wanting
jittery	body feels jumpy
virtuoso	person with great skill or talent
mild jolt	small stimulation
apathy	lack of interest
slurred	unclear

term	definition
staggering drowsy mimic	walking unevenly (drunk) very sleepy imitate

Thinking Critically

Evaluation

The famous sleep researcher Wilse Webb wrote a book called Sleep, the Gentle Tyrant. From what you have learned about sleep, explain why this is or is not a fitting title.

Point/Counterpoint

You hear much debate about the pros and cons of legalizing drugs. Present the most convincing argument possible to support each of these positions:

a. Illicit drugs should be legalized.

b. Illicit drugs should not be legalized.

Psychology in Your Life

You have been asked to make a presentation to Grade 7 and 8 students about the dangers of drugs. What are the most persuasive general arguments you can give to convince them not to get involved with drugs? What are some convincing, specific arguments against using each of these drugs: alcohol, marijuana, cigarettes, and cocaine?

5

LEARNING

CHAPTER OUTLINE

This outline provides a way to organize your notes from both the text and the lecture. It will also serve as a review for the exam.

Module 5A Classical Conditioning	1. Pavlov and Classical Conditioning 2. The Elements and Processes in Classical Conditioning a. The Reflex: We Can't Help It b. The Conditioned and Unconditioned Stimulus and Response c. Extinction and Spontaneous Recovery: Gone But Not Forgotten

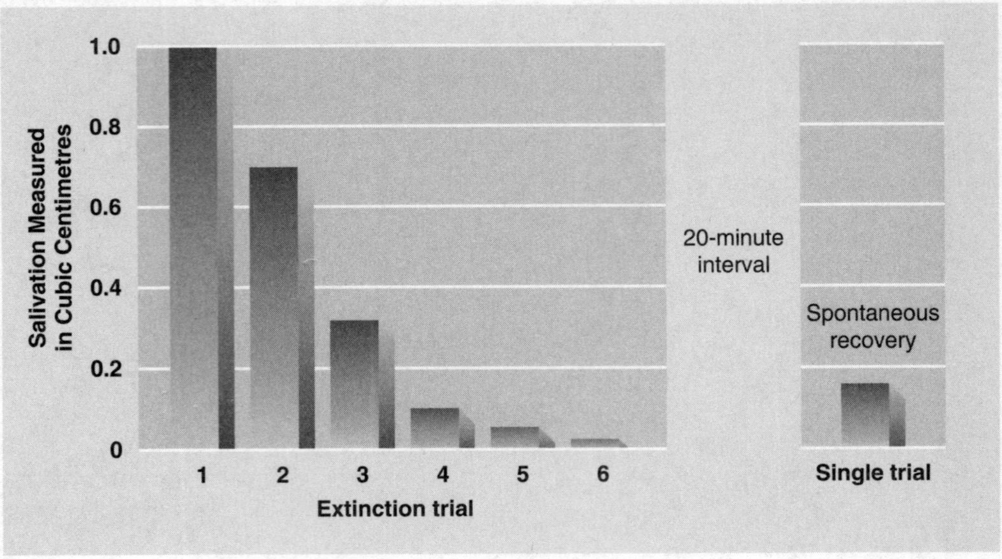

d. Generalization: Responding to Similarities

e. Discrimination: Learning That They're Not All Alike

f. Higher-Order Conditioning

3. John Watson, Little Albert, and Peter

4. Factors Influencing Classical Conditioning

5. Contemporary Views of Classical Conditioning

6. Classical Conditioning in Everyday Life

Module 5B Operant Conditioning	
	1. Skinner and Operant Conditioning
	a. Shaping Behaviour: Just a Little Bit at a Time
	b. Superstitious Behaviour: Mistaking a Coincidence for a Cause
	c. Extinction: Withholding Reinforcers
	d. Generalization and Discrimination
	2. Reinforcement: What's the Payoff?
	a. Positive and Negative Reinforcement: Adding the Good, Taking Away the Bad
	b. Primary and Secondary Reinforcers: The Unlearned and the Learned
	c. Schedules of Reinforcement: When Will I Get My Reinforcers?
	• Fixed-Ratio Schedule
	• Variable-Ratio Schedule
	• Fixed-Interval Schedule
	• Variable-Interval Schedule
	d. The Effect of Continuous and Partial Reinforcement on Extinction
	3. Factors Influencing Operant Conditioning

	4. Punishment: Less Is Best! 5. Escape and Avoidance Learning 6. Learned Helplessness
Module 5C Comparing Classical and Operant Conditioning	1. What Processes Are Comparable In Classical and Operant Conditioning?
Module 5D Behaviour Modification: Changing Our Act	1. What is Behaviour Modification? 2. What Are Token Economies?
Module 5E Cognitive Learning	1. Observational Learning: Watching and Learning a. Learning Aggression: Copying What We See
Apply It!	• How to Win the Battle Against Procrastination

Chapter Learning Objective Questions

Answer the following questions in the space provided and check your answers on the page numbers listed.

5.1 Define learning and classical conditioning. p. 126

5.2 Define and explain each of the key elements of classical conditioning, including US, UR, CS, and CR. p. 127–128

5.3 Understand how basic principles such as extinction, spontaneous recovery, generalization, discrimination, and higher-order conditioning function within classical conditioning. p. 128–130

5.4 Apply classical conditioning theory in a real-world context. p. 131–134

5.5 Identify and explain the factors that influence classical conditioning. p. 131

5.6 Define operant conditioning. p. 136

5.7 Define and explain each of the key elements of operant conditioning, including reinforcers/reinforcement and punishers/punishment. p. 136–139

5.8 Understand how basic principles such as shaping, extinction, spontaneous recovery, generalization, and discrimination function within operant conditioning. p. 138

5.9 Explain how different reinforcement schedules impact on learning. p. 138–141	
5.10 Understand the strengths and weaknesses associated with punishment. p. 142–143	
5.11 Compare and contrast the similarities and differences between classical and operant conditioning and the factors that influence them. p. 144–145	
5.12 Define behaviour modification and token economy. p. 145–147	
5.13 Apply behaviour modification in a real-world context. p. 146	
5.14 Define cognitive learning/observational learning. p. 146	
5.15 Understand the role of observational modelling. p. 147–148	

Study Tips / Try It

Learn to study more effectively and improve your memory with these tips and practical exercises.

Tips on Test Taking

Multiple-choice questions

1. Check the directions to see if the questions call for more than one answer.
2. Answer each question in your head before you look at the possible answers; otherwise you may be confused by the choices.
3. Mark questions you can't answer immediately and come back to them if you have time.
4. If incorrect answers are not deducted from your score, use the following guidelines to guess:
   - If two answers are similar, except for one or two words, choose one of these answers.
   - If two answers have similar sounding or looking words, choose one of these answers.
   - If the answer calls for a sentence completion, eliminate the answers that would not form grammatically correct sentences.
   - If answers cover a numerical range, choose one in the middle.
   - If all else fails, close your eyes and pick one.

True-False Questions

1. Answer these questions quickly.
2. Don't invest a lot of time unless they are worth many points.
3. If any part of the true-false statement is false, the whole statement is false.
4. Absolute qualifiers such as "always" or "never" generally indicate a false statement.

Machine-Graded Tests

1. Check the test against the answer sheet often.
2. Watch for stray marks that look like answers.

Open-Book and Notes Tests

1. Write down key points on a separate sheet.
2. Tape flags onto important pages of the book.
3. Number your notes and write a table of contents.
4. Prepare thoroughly because they are usually the most difficult tests.

Essay Questions

1. Find out precisely what the question is asking. Don't *explain* when asked to *compare.*
2. Make an outline before writing. (Mindmaps work well, see Study Tips Chapter 6.)
3. Be brief, write clearly, use a pen, get to the point, and use examples.

Behavioural Self-Management

1. Choose a target behaviour. Identify the activity you want to change.
2. Record a baseline. Count the number of desired or undesired responses you make each day.
3. Establish goals. Remember the principle of shaping and set realistic goals for gradual improvement in each successive week. Set daily goals that add up to the weekly goal.
4. Choose reinforcers. Set up daily rewards and weekly rewards that are meaningful to you.
5. Record your progress.
6. Collect and enjoy your rewards.
7. Adjust your plan as needed.

Behavioural Contract

If you have trouble sticking with the above steps, try a behavioural contract. In the contract you state a specific problem behaviour you want to control, or a goal you want to achieve. Also state the rewards you will receive, privileges you will forfeit, or punishments you must accept. The contract should be typed and signed by you and a person you trust.

Good Ways to Break Bad Habits

Extinction

Try to discover what is reinforcing a response and remove, avoid, or delay the reinforcement.

Alternate Responses

Try to get the same reinforcement with new responses. For example, if you want to stop smoking but you realize your smoking provides you with your only breaks at work, try taking a walk in the fresh air whenever you want a cigarette.

Cues

Avoid the cues that precede the bad habit you are trying to break. For example, don't walk in the supermarket door by the bakery if you are trying not to eat sweets.

Incompatible Responses

Do something that is incompatible with your bad habit. For example, if you do a jigsaw puzzle while you watch T.V. you can't eat.

What Causes Forgetting?

This is a pertinent question for psychology students given that you are learning new material and you want to be able to remember what you have learned. It could help if you first know what contributes to your forgetting. Two of the main causes of forgetting are:

1. **Encoding Failure**—You don't even encode the information into long-term memory in the first place. This may occur if you assume a passive role in preparing for tests (e.g., merely reading and rereading your text). To avoid encoding failure, test yourself on the material frequently.

2. **Interference**—New information or information you have already learned interferes with the material you are trying to recall. To lessen the effects of interference on memory:

   a. When possible, study before going to sleep.

   b. Review material before going to sleep.

   c. Try not to study subjects back-to-back. Take short breaks between study sessions.

   d. Schedule your classes so that you do not attend courses with similar content back-to-back.

Practice Multiple-Choice Test

After studying the text and completing the Study Guide activities, answer these questions to determine if you need to review any areas before your exam.

1. Learning is any relatively permanent change in behaviour, capability, or attitude that is acquired through:
   a. cognition.
   b. experience.
   c. internal factors.
   d. maturation.

2 Ivan Pavlov, a Nobel Prize-winning physiologist, studied which of the following phenomena?
   a. maturation
   b. animal cognition
   c. operant conditioning
   d. classical conditioning

3. Which of the following is an example of an unconditioned reflex?
   a. Yvette's calling her mother every Sunday afternoon
   b. Josh's startled reaction when a car back-fires
   c. Carole's planting a vegetable garden every May
   d. Heather's turning up the radio whenever a Bruce Springsteen song is being played

4. In Pavlov's original research, dogs heard a tone and then had meat powder placed in their mouths, which caused them to salivate. After many pairings of the tone and the meat powder, they would salivate when the tone was presented alone. In this case, the salivating to the tone is an example of:
   a. a conditioned stimulus.
   b. an unconditioned stimulus.
   c. a conditioned response.
   d. an unconditioned response.

5. Which of the following elements in classical conditioning are learned?
   a. US and UR
   b. US and CR
   c. CS and UR
   d. CS and CR

6. Little Tammy is frightened by thunder and cries when she hears it. During a season of frequent electrical storms, thunder is always preceded by lightning. Now Tammy cries as soon as she sees lightning. In this example, the conditioned response is:
   a. thunder.
   b. lightning.
   c. crying at the sound of thunder.
   d. crying at the sight of lightning.

7. A puff of air on the surface of your eye will make you blink reflexively. If you hear a buzzer repeatedly just before air is puffed into your eye, eventually you will blink as soon as you hear the buzzer. In this example, the unconditioned stimulus is the:
   a. eyeblink response to the buzzer.
   b. buzzer.
   c. puff of air.
   d. eyeblink response to the puff of air.

8. When a conditioned stimulus is repeatedly presented without the unconditioned stimulus:
   a. extinction occurs.
   b. stimulus generalization occurs.
   c. higher-order conditioning occurs.
   d. remission occurs.

9. What key factor led Pavlov to determine that an extinguished conditioned response was not erased or forgotten, but only inhibited?
   a. The conditioned stimulus still appears to create an orienting reflex.
   b. The conditioned response could be recovered in less time than was originally required to learn it.
   c. Brain scans indicated that a permanent change at the synapses had occurred.
   d. The neutral stimulus was no longer neutral.

10. Scott developed a fear of dogs after having been bitten by a collie. The fact that Scott is now fearful of all dogs suggests:
   a. discrimination.
   b. extinction.
   c. spontaneous recovery.
   d. generalization.

11. What is the term for the learned ability to distinguish between similar stimuli so that the conditioned response occurs only to the original conditioned stimulus but not to the similar stimuli?
   a. generalization
   b. discrimination
   c. extinction
   d. spontaneous recovery

12. Advertisers place beautiful people or likeable places and objects with the products they are trying to sell because these items:
   a. distract from the disadvantages of the product.
   b. cause pleasant feelings to be evoked.
   c. are part of the product's basic qualities.
   d. are just elements of scenery.

13. An intense dislike of a particular food associated with nausea or discomfort is known as:
   a. an avoidance learning.
   b. a taste aversion.
   c. higher-order conditioning.
   d. spontaneous recovery.

14. Operant conditioning has been researched most extensively by:
   a. John B. Watson.
   b. Edward Thorndike.
   c. B. F. Skinner.
   d. Ivan Pavlov.

15. In the psychology of learning, any event or object that strengthens or increases the probability of the response it follows is known as:
   a. the law of effect.
   b. a reinforcer.
   c. a punishment.
   d. an aversive stimulus.

16. According to operant conditioning, behaviours change because of the:
   a. involuntary associations formed between stimulus and response.
   b. consequences they produced.
   c. unconscious motivations involved.
   d. observation of other people's behaviours.

17. The technique that teaches complex behaviours by first reinforcing small steps toward the behavioural goal is called:
   a. training.
   b. approximating.
   c. molding.
   d. shaping.

18. What can occur if a person believes that a connection exists between an act and its consequences when there is no relationship between the two?
   a. classical conditioning
   b. superstitious behaviour
   c. shaping
   d. sequential learning

19. According to the principles of operant conditioning, what would be the best way to extinguish temper tantrums in a child?
   a. Punish the child after each temper tantrum.
   b. Punish some of the temper tantrums and ignore the rest.
   c. Never ever give the child what he or she wants during a temper tantrum.
   d. After the tantrum is over, give the child what he or she wanted as a reward for ending the tantrum.

20. An event that increases the probability of a response by removing an unpleasant stimulus is called:
   a. positive reinforcement.
   b. negative reinforcement.
   c. primary reinforcement.
   d. secondary reinforcement.

21. The gold star the teacher gives Tyrone for spelling all the words correctly is a:
   a. contingent reward.
   b. primary reinforcer.
   c. discriminative stimulus.
   d. secondary reinforcer.

22. The following are factors which affect the strength of a classically conditioned fear response and the length of time for conditioning EXCEPT:
   a. the intensity of the UCS
   b. the number of pairings of the CR and the UCR
   c. how reliably the CS predicts the UCS
   d. the temporal relationship between the CS and the UCS

23. In operant conditioning, the ____________ of behaviour are manipulated to increase or decrease the frequency of a response or to shape and entirely new response.
   a. elements
   b. approximations
   c. consequences
   d. baseline

24. ____________________ is the systemic application of the learning principles of operant conditioning, classical conditioning or observational learning to individuals or groups in order to eliminate undesirable behaviour and/or encourage desirable behaviour.
   a. learning methodology
   b. behaviour approximations
   c. learned application
   d. behaviour modification

25. A ____________________ is a program that motivates and reinforces socially acceptable behaviours with tokens that can be exchanged for desired items or privileges.
   a. learning methodology
   b. baseline
   c. token economy
   d. behavioural contract

Answers to Multiple-Choice Questions

Question Number	Answer	Explanation for application questions
1.	b.	
2.	d.	
3.	b.	We are born with reacting to loud noises, which means the car backfiring is an unconditioned stimulus.
4.	c.	
5.	d.	
6.	d.	Tammy had to learn to be afraid of the lightning because it was associated with a loud noise. Conditioned responses are learned.
7.	c.	
8.	a.	
9.	b.	
10.	d.	Generalization occurs when we generalize our reaction to similar stimuli.
11.	b.	
12.	b.	
13.	b.	
14.	c.	
15.	b.	
16.	b.	
17.	d.	
18.	b.	Superstitious behaviour occurs when we believe two things are related even when they are not.
19.	c.	
20.	b.	
21.	d.	Primary reinforcers are rewards that directly meet needs, such as food and water. Secondary reinforcers enable us to meet needs indirectly.
22.	b.	
23.	b.	
24.	d.	
25.	c.	

Glossary for Text Language Enhancement

Students identified the following words from the text as needing more explanation. This page can be cut out, folded in half, and used as a bookmark for this chapter.

term	definition
vicious	mean
extortion	using threat of force to take money from someone
reign of terror	a time during which many people are hurt
maturation	process of becoming fully grown
exclude	reject
infer	deduce from evidence
incision	cut
different avenues	various ways
meticulous	very exact and careful
hermetically	perfectly airtight
girders	beams
embedded	buried
moat	trench around building
vibrations	back and forward movement
adjoining	connected
puff of air	quick and forceful movement of air
buzzers	make "zzzzz" sounds
striking	hitting
acquisition	to gain or acquire
formulated	created
phenomenon	a notable thing
sanction	approve
drug-craving	very powerfully desiring drugs
drug paraphernalia	things used to take drugs
steel	a very strong metal
elicit	make happen
optimal	best
aversion	wanting to avoid
emitted	gave off or performed
food pellets	small hard food pieces
disruptive	disturbing
amazing feats	impressive acts
temper tantrum	act out violently
erratic	not the usual or expected
disks	circles
peck	hit with beak
unwittingly	without knowing
nagging	constant complaining
magnitude	size

term	definition
in conjunction with	along with
discharging anger	getting rid of anger
token	something that has an agreed-upon worth, for exchange
consciousness raising	making people aware of something
pervasiveness	being everywhere
Bobo Doll	inflatable punching bag

Thinking Critically

Evaluation

Prepare statements outlining the strengths and limitations of classical conditioning, operant conditioning, and observational learning in explaining how behaviours are acquired and maintained.

Point/Counterpoint

The use of behaviour modification has been a source of controversy among psychologists and others. Prepare arguments supporting each of the following positions:

a. Behaviour modification should be used in society to shape the behaviour of others.
b. Behaviour modification should not be used in society to shape the behaviour of others.

Psychology in Your Life

Think of a behaviour of a friend, a family member, or a professor that you would like to change. Using what you know about classical conditioning, operant conditioning, and observational learning, formulate a detailed plan for changing the behaviour of the target person.

6

MEMORY

CHAPTER OUTLINE

This outline provides a way to organize your notes from both the text and the lecture. It will also serve as a review for the exam.

Module 6A Remembering

1. The Three Processes in Memory: Encoding, Storage, and Retrieval

The Processes Required in Remembering

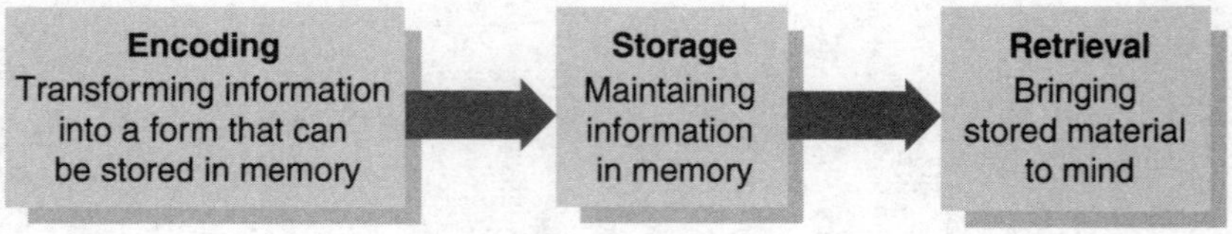

2. Information-Processing Approach: The Three Memory Systems

The Three Memory Systems

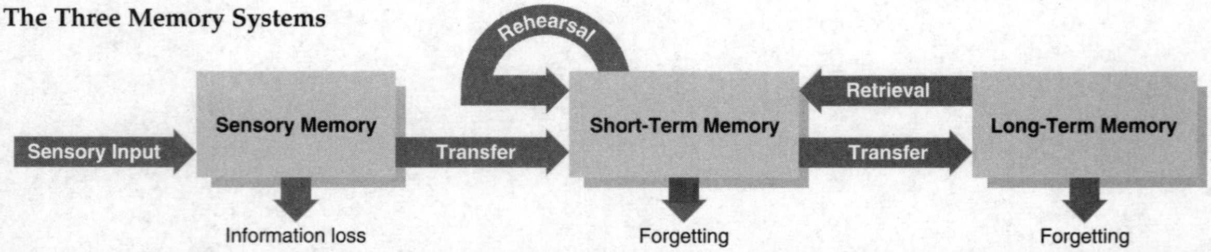

Subsystems of Long-Term Memory

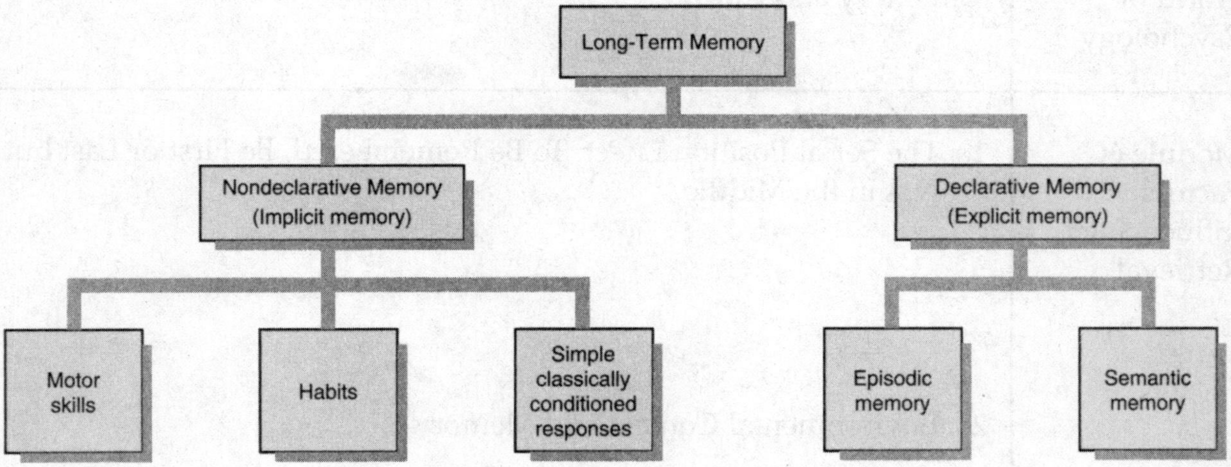

3. The Levels-of-Processing Model: Another View of Memory

4. Measuring Memory

   Three methods:

   1. Recall
   2. Recognition
   3. The Relearning Method

Module 6B
The Nature of Remembering

1. Memory as a Permanent Record: The Video Recorder Analogy

2. Memory as a Reconstruction: Partly Fact and Partly Fiction

3. Eyewitness Testimony: Is It Accurate?

4. Recovering Repressed Memories: A Controversy

5. Unusual Memory Phenomena

World of Psychology	• Memory and Culture
Module 6C Factors Influencing Retrieval	1. The Serial Position Effect: To Be Remembered, Be First or Last but Not in the Middle 2. Environmental Context and Memory 3. The State-Dependent Memory Effect
Module 6D Biology and Memory	1. Brain Damage: A Clue to Memory Formation 2. Neuronal Changes in Memory: Brain Work 3. Hormones and Memory

Module 6E
Forgetting

1. Hermann Ebbinghaus and the First Experimental Studies on Learning and Memory

Ebbinghaus's Curve of Forgetting

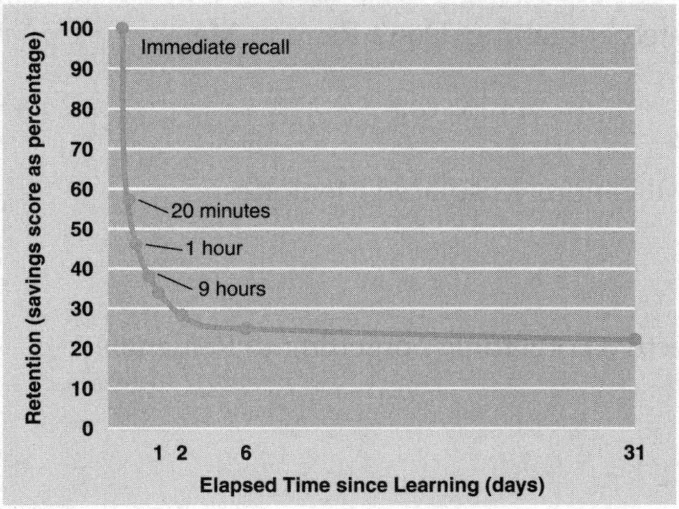

2. The Causes of Forgetting

   a. Encoding Failure

   b. Decay

   c. Interference

Retroactive and Proactive Interference

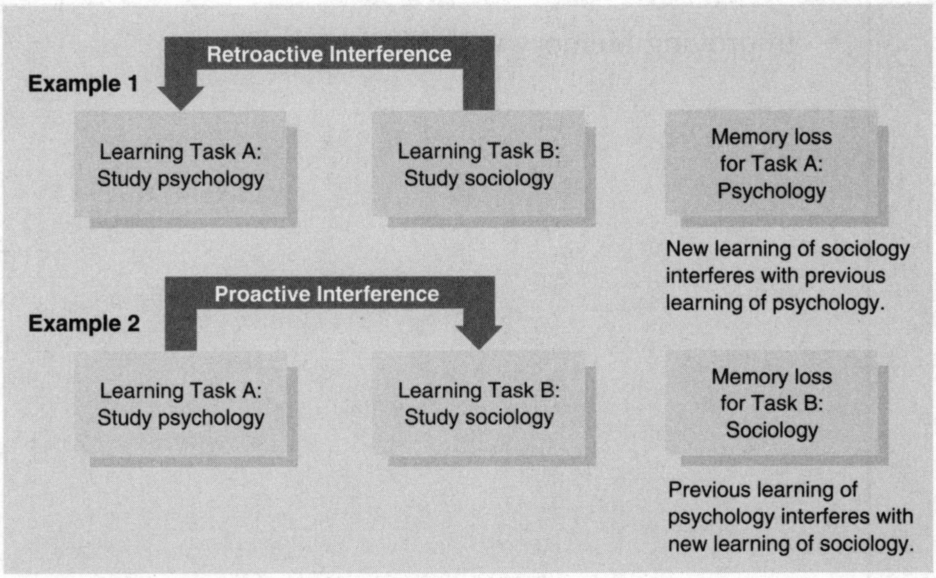

	d. Consolidation Failure e. Motivated Forgetting: Don't Remind Me f. Retrieval Failure: Misplaced Memories g. Prospective Forgetting: Forgetting to Remember
Module 6F Improving Memory	1. Study Habits That Aid Memory
Apply It!	• Improving Memory with Mnemonic Devices

Chapter Learning Objective Questions

Answer the following questions in the space provided and check your answers on the page numbers listed.

6.1 Identify and define the three memory processes: encoding, storage and retrieval. p. 156	
6.2 Define and explain the functioning of each component of the Atkinson-Shiffrin model of memory, including sensory, short-term, and long-term memory. p. 156–161	
6.3 Explain how the levels-of-processing model accounts for memory. p. 160	
6.4 Define and understand the types of long-term memory: declarative and non-declarative. p. 160–161	
6.5 Compare and contrast the three methods of measuring memory: recall, recognition and relearning. p. 160–161	
6.6 Explain what is meant when memory is described as a reconstructive process. p. 163	
6.7 Define and explain what schemas are and do. p. 164–165	
6.8 Describe factors that can limit or enhance accuracy of eyewitness testimony. p. 165	
6.9 Understand the strengths and weaknesses associated with hypnosis. p. 166	

6.10 Define and describe the serial position effect, including primacy and recency effects. p. 169

6.11 Explain how the environmental context impacts on retrieval. p. 169

6.12 Define state-dependent memory. p. 170

6.13 Understand how exceptional cases of memory loss help us to understand memory processes and functioning. p. 171

6.14 Understand the role of the hippocampus, prefrontal lobe, and hormones for memory. p. 171–173

6.15 Define anterograde amnesia and long-term potentiation and explain their role in memory. p. 172

6.16 Define and explain the following seven causes of forgetting: encoding failure, decay, interference, consolidation failure, motivated forgetting, retrieval failure, and prospective forgetting. p. 174–176

6.17 Identify and define four study habits that aid memory. p. 177

6.18 Compare the learning outcomes of overlearning, spaced versus massed practice, and active learning versus rereading. p. 178

Chart Completion

Fill in the Information in the White Blocks

The Processes Required in Remembering

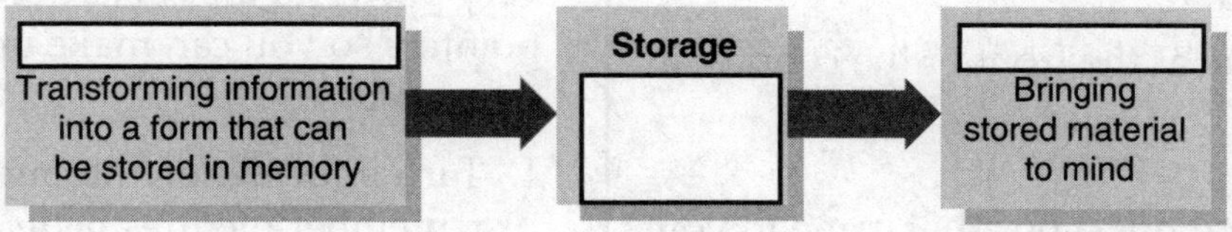

The Three Memory Systems

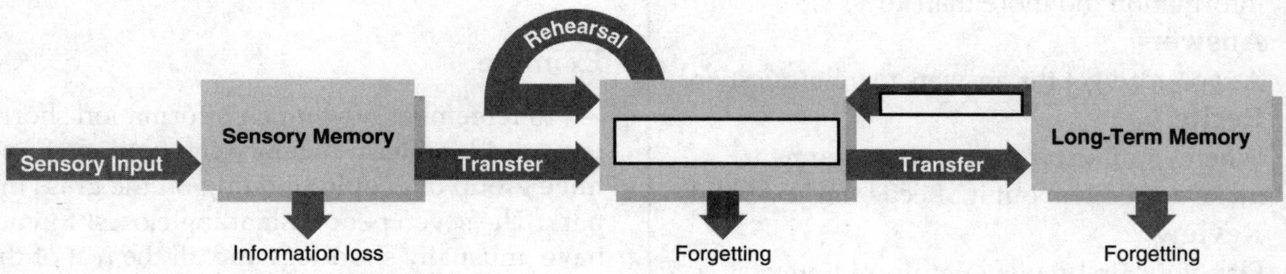

Subsystems of Long-Term Memory

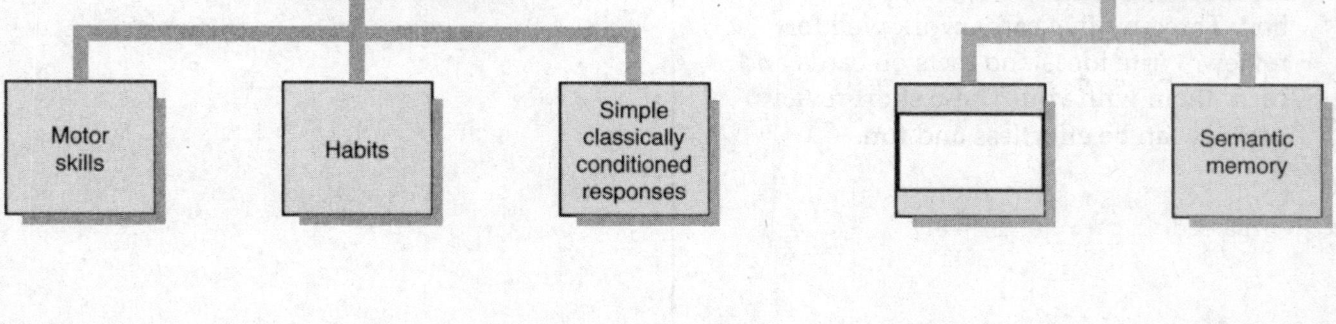

Study Tips / Try It

Learn to study more effectively and improve your memory with these tips and practical exercises.

Reading for Remembering

1. **Skim**
   Skim the entire chapter.
2. **Outline**
   Read the outline at the front of the chapter in the text.
3. **Questions**
   Write out several questions that come to your mind that you think will be answered in the chapter.
4. **Read** the material.
5. **Highlight**
   While reading, highlight the most important information (no more than 10%).
6. **Answers**
   As you read get the answers to your questions.
7. **Recite**
   When you finish reading an assignment, make a speech about it. Recite the key points.
8. **Review**
   Plan your first review within 24 hours.
9. **Review again**
   Weekly reviews are important—perhaps only four or five minutes per assignment. Go over your notes. Read the highlighted parts of your text. Recite the more complicated points.

More about Review

You can do short reviews any time, anywhere, if you are prepared. Take your text to the dentist's office, and if you don't have time to read a whole assignment, review last week's assignment. Conduct five-minute reviews when you are waiting for water to boil. Three-by-five cards work well for review. Write ideas and facts on cards and carry them with you. These short review periods can be effortless and fun.

Try Your Own Mnemonics

Chapter 6 in your textbook discusses mnemonics. Most memory experts agree that mnemonics are very powerful tools. Here are some additional pointers so you can make up your own mnemonics.

1. Turn information into mental pictures. We remember pictures better than words, and the funnier or more unusual the better.

2. Make things meaningful to you.

3. Connect the information to what you already know.

Example

To remember how much information short-term and long-term memory can hold, picture a huge group of people standing on the grass in a park. The seven people standing closest to you have unusually short legs and all the rest of the people have unusually long legs. (Remember we said funny is good.) The short-legged people represent the fact that we are able to hold an average of 7 items in short-term memory. The many long-legged people represent that long-term memory is practically unlimited.

Now think of one of your own and write it here.

Practice Multiple-Choice Test

After studying the text and completing the Study Guide activities, answer these questions to determine if you need to review any areas before your exam.

1. To transform sensory input into a form that is more readily processed by one's memory is to __________ the input.
   a. retrieve
   b. chunk
   c. rehearse
   d. encode

2. The second stage of information processing for memory maintenance is:
   a. encoding.
   b. storage.
   c. retrieval.
   d. episodic.

3. The memory process of locating and returning stored information to the conscious state is referred to as:
   a. encoding.
   b. procedural encoding.
   c. storage.
   d. retrieval.

4. An usher points out a seat to Paul in a darkened theatre by moving a flashlight in a rectangular motion. Paul sees the form of the rectangle because images from the flashlight are being briefly stored in his:
   a. semantic memory.
   b. short-term memory.
   c. photographic memory.
   d. sensory memory.

5. Working memory is another term for:
   a. iconic memory.
   b. semantic memory.
   c. elaborative rehearsal.
   d. short-term memory.

6. In the ______ memory the stimulus tends to fade significantly after 20 to 30 seconds if it is not repeated.
   a. iconic and echoic
   b. sensory
   c. long-term
   d. short-term

7. Jamie meets someone at a party and wants to remember his name. To do this, she repeats his name over and over in her mind. This process is called:
   a. rehearsal.
   b. consolidation.
   c. categorization.
   d. indexing.

8. The memory of events experienced by a person is known as:
   a. procedural memory.
   b. semantic memory.
   c. iconic memory.
   d. episodic memory.

9. When another student tells you that he knows the three kinds of memory, he is using:
   a. semantic memory.
   b. episodic memory.
   c. procedural memory.
   d. metamemory.

10. Knowledge and memory of the steps involved in riding a bicycle are a result of __________ memory.
    a. echoic
    b. implicit
    c. semantic
    d. episodic

11. The short-term memory can hold ______ chunks of information at any one time.
    a. 3
    b. 7
    c. 10
    d. 12

12. The type(s) of memory capable of virtually permanent storage is the:
    a. long-term memory.
    b. short-term memory.
    c. sensory memory.
    d. iconic and echoic memories.

13. The easiest type of memory task is:
   a. recall.
   b. recognition.
   c. relearning.
   d. savings.

14. Multiple-choice tests such as this one measure _____ memory tasks.
   a. recall
   b. recognition
   c. relearning
   d. savings

15. The method of savings is used to investigate:
   a. recall.
   b. readiness.
   c. recognition.
   d. relearning.

16. According to Ebbinghaus's curve of forgetting, forgetting occurs most rapidly:
   a. approximately 31 days after learning.
   b. immediately after the material is learned.
   c. during the learning process.
   d. during stress.

17. In psychoanalytic theory, the ejection of anxiety-evoking ideas from our conscious awareness is called:
   a. elaborative rehearsal.
   b. displacement.
   c. repression.
   d. regression.

18. We may forget because of experiences that occur before or after learning something new according to the:
   a. decay theory.
   b. interference theory.
   c. motivation theory.
   d. engram theory.

19. Justin believes that we reconstruct our recollections by elaborating on pieces of information. Mike argues that our recollections are like accurate snapshots in our long-term memories. Carla states that we have faithful mental representation in our long-term memories.
   a. Justin is correct.
   b. Mike is correct.
   c. Carla is correct.
   d. All the above are correct.

20. Remembering in detail where you were and what you were doing when the news broke that the space shuttle *Challenger* had exploded would represent what memory experts call:
   a. flashbulb memory.
   b. episodic memory.
   c. state-dependent memory.
   d. eidetic memory.

21. If you visited your old high school building, you might recall events that occurred there much more easily. This type of memory stimulation is known as:
   a. environmental context.
   b. state-dependent memory.
   c. photographic memory.
   d. iconic memory.

22. When people feel anger, they may be reminded of other times of anger and frustration. This type of memory is known as:
   a. metamemory.
   b. working memory.
   c. context-dependent memory.
   d. state-dependent memory.

23. In the case of H. M., his operation prevented him from transferring information from his
   a. sensory memory to his short-term memory.
   b. short-term memory to his long-term memory.
   c. iconic memory to his acoustic memory.
   d. procedural memory to his semantic memory.

24. The _____ is a structure in the limbic system that plays an important role in the formation of new memories.
   a. thalamus
   b. Broca's area
   c. hippocampus
   d. parietal lobe

25. In a list of words, we would probably remember:
   a. the first and middle words.
   b. the first and last words.
   c. the middle and last words.
   d. just the middle words.

Answers to Multiple-Choice Questions

Question Number	Answer	Explanation for application questions
1.	d.	
2.	b.	
3.	d.	Retrieval involves locating and retrieving stored information.
4.	d.	Sensory memory holds onto sensations for a very brief period of time.
5.	d.	Working memory and short-term memory are equivalent terms.
6.	d.	Short-term memory only lasts a few seconds if we do not rehearse.
7.	a.	Repeating something over and over is called rehearsal.
8.	d.	Episodic memory refers to remembering the"episodes" of our lives.
9.	a.	Semantic memory stores information like a dictionary.
10.	b.	Implicit memory contains memories of skills we have learned.
11.	b.	Short-term memory can hold about 7 items or chunks.
12.	a.	Long-term memory can hold onto an unlimited amount of information virtually forever.
13.	b.	It is easiest to recognize information.
14.	b.	Multiple-choice questions mainly require recognition.
15.	d.	
16	b.	Retention goes down dramatically after the first 9 hours.
17.	c.	Elaborative rehearsal helps memory.
18.	b.	
19.	a.	
20.	a.	
21.	a.	The context is giving the retrieval cues.
22.	d.	Internal physiology and emotions can serve as retrieval cues. This is called state-dependent learning.
23.	b.	H. M. (case study in your textbook) could not transfer short-term memory into long-term memory.
24.	c.	Hippocampus is important in the formation of new memories.
25.	b.	We remember the first and last items on lists.

Glossary for Text Language Enhancement

Students identified the following words from the text as needing more explanation.
This page can be cut out, folded in half, and used as a bookmark for this chapter.

term	definition
stab	put a knife into
astonishing	surprising and shocking
alibi	the fact of being somewhere else when a crime was committed
rustling	moving about making noise
fades	becomes less easy to recall
disrupted	interfered with
floppy disk	disk for computer
analogy	similarity
discrete	separate
ingenious	good and useful
abundance	a large amount
acoustic form	by sound
chunks	larger pieces
rehearsal	repeating over and over
distraction	pulls attention away
semantic	meaning of something
repetitive	repeating
shallowest	opposite of deepest
retention	memory
cues	signs to help connection
to jog	help
seizure	convulsive fit
hinder	prevent
dashboard	panel of gauges in a car
haunt	keep coming to mind
flashbacks	strong memories
replica	copy
expectation	what a person thinks will happen
distort	change and bend
distortion	something that is changed
infallible	never wrong
hypnotized	in a trance-like state of consciousness
skeptical	uncertain something is truthful
vivid	strong and clear
constitute	make up
reinstated	brought back
intoxicated	drunk
sober	not drunk

term	definition
amphetamines	drugs that speed up
barbiturates	drugs that calm down
synapses	communication between nerve cells
haphazard	not organized
cramming	studying at last minute

Thinking Critically

Evaluation

Some studies cited in this chapter involved only one or a few participants.

a. Select two of these studies and discuss the possible problems in drawing conclusions on the basis of studies using so few participants.

b. Suggest several possible explanations for the researchers' findings other than those proposed by the researchers.

c. In your view, should such studies even be mentioned in a textbook? Why or why not?

Point/Counterpoint

Using what you have learned in this chapter on memory, prepare an argument citing cases and specific examples to support each of these positions:

a. Long-term memory is a permanent record of our experiences.

b. Long-term memory is not necessarily a permanent record of our experiences.

Psychology in Your Life

Drawing upon your knowledge, formulate a plan that you can put into operation to help improve your memory and avoid the pitfalls that cause forgetting.

7

COGNITION, LANGUAGE, AND INTELLIGENCE

CHAPTER OUTLINE

This outline provides a way to organize your notes from both the text and the lecture. It will also serve as a review for the exam.

Module 7A Cognition	1. Imagery and Concepts: Tools of Thinking 2. Imagery: Picture This—Elephants with Purple Polka Dots 3. Concepts: Our Mental Classification System (Is a Penguin a Bird?)

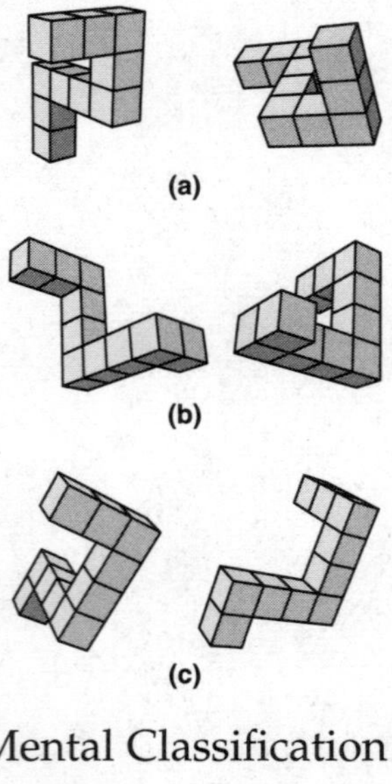

	4. Decision Making: Getting an Answer 5. Problem Solving: How Do We Begin? a. Trial and Error b. Algorithms c. Heuristic Strategies in Problem Solving 6. Impediments to Problem Solving: Mental Stumbling Blocks a. Functional Fixedness b. Mental Set
Module 7B Creativity: Unique and Useful Productions	a. Creativity and Intelligence: How Do They Relate?
Module 7C Language	1. The Structure of Language • Phonemes • Morphemes • Syntax • Semantics 2. Language Development • Cooing and Babbling • The One-Word Stage

	• The Two-Word Stage and Telegraphic Speech • Suffixes, Function Words, and Grammatical Rules 3. Theories of Language Development: How Do We Acquire It? • Learning Theory • The Nativist Position • The Interactionist Perspective 4. Having More Than One Language 5. Animal Language 6. Language and Thinking
Apply It!	• Building A Powerful Vocabulary 1. Think Analytically 2. Word Connections 3. Knowledge of Word Parts
Module 7D The Nature of Intelligence	1. The Search for Factors Underlying Intelligence a. Spearman and General Intelligence: The *g* Factor b. Thurstone's Primary Mental Abilities: Primarily Seven c. Guilford's Structure of Intellect: A Mental House with 180 Rooms 2. Intelligence: More Than One Type? a. Gardner's Theory of Multiple Intelligences: Eight Frames of Mind

b. Sternberg's Triarchic Theory of Intelligence: The Big Three

Module 7E Measuring Intelligence

1. Alfred Binet and the First Successful Intelligence Test

2. The Intelligence Quotient, or IQ

$$\frac{\text{Mental Age}}{\text{Chronological Age}} \times 100 = \text{IQ}$$

3. Intelligence Testing in North America

a. The Stanford-Binet Intelligence Scale

b. Intelligence Testing for Adults

c. The Wechsler Intelligence Tests

d. Group Intelligence Tests

4. Requirements of Good Tests: Reliability, Validity, and Standardization

a. Reliability

b. Validity

c. Standardization

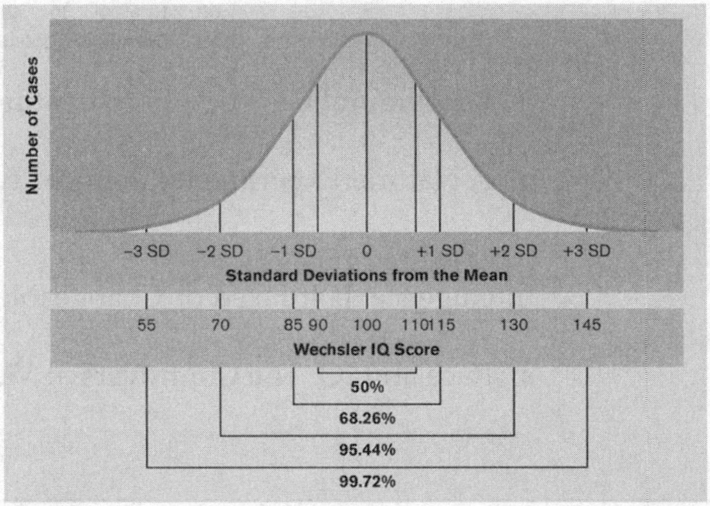

Module 7F The Range of Intelligence

a. Terman's Study of Gifted People: 1528 Geniuses and How They Grew

b. Who Is Gifted?

c. Understanding Mental Retardation/Intellectual Deficits

Module 7G The IQ Controversy: Brainy Dispute	1. The Uses and Abuses of Intelligence Tests a. Intelligence Test Scores: Can they predict success and failure? b. The abuses of intelligence tests: Making too much of a single number 2. The Nature–Nurture Controversy: Battle of the Centuries

Correlations between the IQ Scores of Persons with Various Relationships

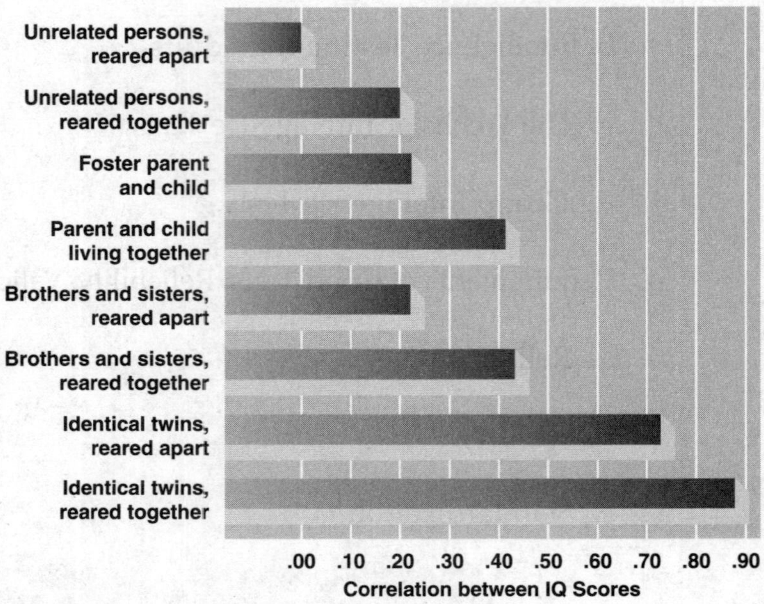

a. Behavioural Genetics: Investigating Nature and Nurture

b. A Natural Experiment: Identical Twins Reared Apart

3. Intelligence: Is It Fixed or Changeable?

a. Race and IQ: The Controversial Views

Module 7H Emotional Intelligence	1. Personal Components of Emotional Intelligence 2. Interpersonal Components of Emotional Intelligence

Chapter Learning Objective Questions

Answer the following questions in the space provided and check your answers on the page numbers listed.

7.1 Define cognition, imagery, concept, prototype, exemplars, and heuristics. p. 186–188	
7.2 What are roles of systematic processes, heuristics, framing, intuition, and anchoring in decision making? p. 188–189	
7.3 Compare trial and error versus algorithm methods for problem solving. p. 190	
7.4 Explain means-end analysis and working backward. p. 191	
7.5 Describe two barriers to problem solving. p. 191–192	
7.6 Define creativity. p. 192	
7.7 Explain the role of divergent thinking in creativity. p. 192	
7.8 Define language and psycholinguistics. p. 193	
7.9 Identify the elements of language, and generate an English language example for each element. p. 194	

7.10 Identify the progression of the development of language. p. 194–195

7.11 Explain how learning theory and the nativist position account for the acquisition of language. p. 195–196

7.12 Understand the similarities and differences between human and primate language. p. 197-198

7.13 Identify the factors underlying intelligence as defined by Spearman, Thurstone, and Guilford. p. 200

7.14 Contrast the differences among factors underlying intelligence. p. 200

7.15 Identify Gardner's and Sternberg's types of intelligences. p. 201–202

7.16 List the different kind of IQ tests. p. 203

7.17 Describe how intelligence is assessed by each test. p. 203–204

7.18 Explain what is required for a test to be a good measure of intelligence. p. 204–205

7.19 Define and describe what is meant by norms and deviation scores. p. 205

7.20 Describe the outcomes of Terman's longitudinal study of intelligence. p. 205

7.21 Define giftedness. p. 205

7.22 Define retardation and explain the implications for individuals at each level of retardation. p. 206

7.23 Understand the relative contributions of nature and nurture for IQ. p. 207–208

7.24 Define heritability. p. 208

7.25 Describe and explain the Flynn effect on IQ. p. 210

7.26 Define and explain emotional intelligence. p. 211–212

Study Tips   Try It

Learn to study more effectively and improve your memory with these tips and practical exercises.

Anxiety Interferes with Performance

Do you freeze up on exams, worried that you won't do well? We can turn one exam into a "do or die" catastrophic situation. Yes, we should try our best, but we are not doomed for life if we fail at something. Perhaps the following examples will help you see a failure for what it is, just one more step in the process of life.

- Einstein was four years old before he could speak and seven before he could read.
- Isaac Newton did poorly in grade school.
- Beethoven's music teacher once said of him, "As a composer he is hopeless."
- When Thomas Edison was a boy, his teachers told him he was too stupid to learn anything.
- Woolworth got a job in a dry goods store when he was 21, but his employers would not let him wait on a customer because he "didn't have enough sense."
- A newspaper editor fired Walt Disney because he had "no good ideas."
- Leo Tolstoy flunked out of college.
- Louis Pasteur was rated as "mediocre" in chemistry when he attended college.
- Abraham Lincoln entered the Black Hawk War as a captain and came out as a private.
- Winston Churchill failed the sixth grade.

Failures mean very little in the big picture of our lives. It is just important that we keep trying.

Problem-Solving Technique

Try the technique outlined below on a problem in your own life.

Technique	Your Problem
Stage 1 Describe problem	
Stage 2 Generate possible solutions	
Stage 3 Evaluate solutions	
Stage 4 Try solutions, evaluate results	
Revisions Try new solutions, evaluate results	

Study Habits That Aid Memory

All learners are not created equal. Still, there are habits and skills that can aid the memory process when learning new material such as that in your text.

1. **Organization**—It is best to organize the material you are committing to memory in a meaningful way. When you go looking for it, it will be easier to find.
2. **Overlearning**—Don't stop studying when you think you know the material. Go over it again and again until it feels like you more than know it. You will remember more when test time comes if you overlearn the material.
3. **Spaced versus Massed Practice**—Study a little bit every day for the duration of your course. For example, if you study every day for 0.5 hours, you will be more likely to recall the material than if you study 3.5 hours (i.e., the same massed time) once per week.
4. **Active Learning versus Rereading**—Be on a quest for answers when you approach the material. Seek to actively learn the answers to your questions as opposed to passively reading the text. It will make a difference at recall time.

Find Your EQ

Emotional intelligence may be just as important to success in your academic career as your actual academic skills. Take this short test to assess your EQ. Check one response for each statement.

1. I am always aware of even subtle feelings as I have them.

___Always ___Usually ___Sometimes

___Rarely ___Never

2. I can delay gratification in pursuit of my goals instead of getting carried away by impulse.

___Always ___Usually ___Sometimes

___Rarely ___Never

3. Instead of giving up in the face of setbacks or disappointments, I stay hopeful and optimistic.

___Always ___Usually ___Sometimes

___Rarely ___Never

4. My keen sense of others' feelings makes me compassionate about their plight.

___Always ___Usually ___Sometimes

___Rarely ___Never

5. I can sense the pulse of a group or relationship and state unspoken feelings.

___Always ___Usually ___Sometimes

___Rarely ___Never

6. I can soothe or contain distressing feelings so that they don't keep me from doing the things I need to do.

___Always ___Usually ___Sometimes

___Rarely ___Never

Score your responses as follows:
Always = 4 points, Usually = 3 points, Sometimes = 2 points, Rarely = 1 point, Never = 0 points. The closer your total number of points is to 24, the higher your EQ probably is.

Practice Multiple-Choice Test

After studying the text and completing the Study Guide activities, answer these questions to determine if you need to review any areas before your exam.

1. The first intelligence test was developed by ____ as a means of identifying children who could not benefit from regular education.
   a. Binet
   b. Terman
   c. Stanford
   d. Wechsler

2. On an intelligence test, a 5-year-old child is able to answer the questions that the average 6-year-old can answer. The child's IQ is:
   a. 120.
   b. 125.
   c. 100.
   d. 95.

3. According to the original formula for IQ, if a person's mental age and chronological age were equal, IQ would be:
   a. zero.
   b. one.
   c. 100.
   d. 110.

4. The Wechsler scales are made up of two basic subtest divisions. They are the ________ and the ______ divisions.
   a. verbal; performance
   b. verbal; information
   c. performance; mathematical
   d. vocabulary; information

5. A test is said to be reliable if it:
   a. measures what it says it measures.
   b. gives consistent results when a person is retested.
   c. tests many different abilities.
   d. does not show racial and ethnic differences in scores.

6. If a test measures what it is supposed to measure, it is said to be:
   a. reliable.
   b. valid.
   c. culture-free.
   d. cognitively complex.

7. In order to standardize a test,
   a. compose items that reflect the knowledge and behaviours of experts in the quality being tested.
   b. give subjects half the test items on one occasion and the other half on another, and compare consistency.
   c. arrange items to reflect the predictions of a psychological theory.
   d. administer it to a large number of people who represent the population for which the test was designed, and examine their scores.

8. What is the average IQ score in the Stanford-Binet and Wechsler?
   a. 50
   b. 75
   c. 100
   d. 150

9. What myths about gifted people did Terman's study disprove?
   a. Mentally superior people are likely to be physically inferior.
   b. There's a thin line between genius and madness.
   c. Gifted people don't have common sense.
   d. All of the above

10. Who was the theorist who suggested that the behaviours considered to be intelligent have a common factor called "general intelligence"?
    a. Sternberg
    b. Spearman
    c. Binet
    d. Terman

11. According to Sternberg's triarchic theory of intelligence, behaviour that permits people to adapt to the demands of their environment is intelligence called:
    a. contextual.
    b. experiential.
    c. componential.
    d. metacomponents.

12. Sternberg's model of intelligence differs from the traditional models in that Sternberg believes that:
   a. intelligence is inherited.
   b. intelligence includes how people function in the real world.
   c. IQ tests are biased toward minorities.
   d. there is only one kind of intelligence.

13. IQ tests are:
   a. good predictors of success in school.
   b. good predictors of success in life but not in school.
   c. good predictors of motivation but not success.
   d. poorly correlated with any other measure of achievement.

14. Many psychologists believe that the IQ tests in current use are:
   a. culture-free.
   b. unreliable.
   c. biased in favour of minorities.
   d. biased in favour of the white middle class.

15. Studies have found a stronger relationship between IQ scores of adopted children and their ________ parents than with their ________ parents.
   a. adoptive; grand-
   b. biological; grand-
   c. biological; adoptive
   d. adoptive; biological

16. The best way to assess the relative contributions of heredity and environment is to:
   a. compare identical and fraternal twins.
   b. study identical twins who have been separated at birth and reared apart.
   c. study fraternal twins who have been separated at birth and reared apart.
   d. study children who were adopted at birth by comparing them to their biological and adoptive parents.

17. In Emotional Intelligence, managing emotions means to:
   a. give free rein to every feeling and impulse.
   b. express emotions in an appropriate manner.
   c. suppress our emotions in public.
   d. display only positive emotional moods.

18. With the ________ approach to problem-solving, you try various solutions until, perhaps, one will work.
   a. analogy
   b. algorithm
   c. heuristic
   d. trial-and-error

19. Using a mental set to solve a problem refers to our tendency to:
   a. stand back from a problem.
   b. use set procedures that guarantee success.
   c. use techniques that worked in the past.
   d. use means–end analysis.

20. The tendency to view an object in terms of its familiar usage is defined as:
   a. mental set.
   b. incubation.
   c. functional fixedness.
   d. algorithmic perception.

21. The ability to generate novel solutions to problems, characterized by originality, ingenuity, and flexibility, is referred to as:
   a. creativity.
   b. intelligence.
   c. algorithmic activity.
   d. heuristic thinking.

22. A 2-year-old calling every car, bus, truck, and motorcycle a "car" illustrates:
   a. overregularization.
   b. overextension.
   c. mental combinations.
   d. mental representation.

23. Which of the following factors contributes to creativity?
   a. originality
   b. dependency
   c. conformity
   d. inhibition

24. Which of the following is an interpersonal component of Emotional Intelligence?
   a. being self-motivated.
   b. an ability to postpone immediate gratification.
   c. managing our inner feelings about others.
   d. an ability to handle relationships.

25. Peters (1995) and Winston (1996) have challenged the allegations of J. Philippe Rushton that races could be ranked in order of intelligence. They questioned:

a. Rushton's methodology.
b. the accuracy of his measurement.
c. whether the studies actually tested intelligence.
d. all of the above.

26. A study of children conceived during WWII (Eyeferth, 1961) showed that:

a. Rushton's methodology was corrupt.
b. having a black father conferred a measurable IQ advantage.
c. having a white father conferred a measurable IQ advantage.
d. having a white father conferred no measurable IQ advantage at all.

Answers to Multiple-Choice Questions

Question Number	Answer	Explanation for application questions
1.	a.	
2.	a.	$IQ = \frac{\text{mental age}}{\text{chronological age}} \times 100$ $\frac{6}{5} \times 100 = 120$
3.	c.	$\frac{\text{mental age}}{\text{chronological age}} = 1 \times 100 = 100$
4.	a.	Wechsler scales are the verbal and performance.
5.	b.	
6.	b.	
7.	d.	Standardization is defined in response d.
8.	c.	The average IQ is 100 for both Stanford-Binet and Wechsler.
9.	d.	Terman disproved all three of the myths listed in the responses.
10.	b.	Spearman believed there was a common factor "g."
11.	a.	Sternberg's theory consisted of componential (IQ score), experiential (insight), and contextual (common sense).
12.	b.	Sternberg was interested in how a person functioned in the environment.
13.	a.	IQ tests are similar to school exams, so IQ test performance can predict school success.
14.	d.	Most IQ tests use the vocabulary of the white middle class and therefore favour them.
15.	c.	IQ scores are closer in blood relatives as compared with non-related people living together.
16.	b.	
17.	b.	
18.	d.	
19.	c.	A mental set interferes with our openness to new ideas because it is a focus on techniques that worked in the past.
20.	c.	
21.	a.	The question describes creativity.
22.	b.	Inappropriately applying the grammatical rules for forming plurals and past tenses to irregular nouns.
23.	a.	
24.	d.	
25.	d.	Guelph University researchers brought forward major concerns over Rushton's research
26.	d.	The results were obtained by comparing IQs of children with black fathers with children with white fathers.

Glossary for Text Language Enhancement

Students identified the following words from the text as needing more explanation. This page can be cut out, folded in half, and used as a bookmark for this chapter.

term	definition
legacy	something passed on by a predecessor
genius	very intelligent
prominent	important
labelled	said to be
dunce	not smart
tap	connect with
dexterity	ability
formulated	put together
deficient	not as good as expected
flaw	mistake
highly regarded	thought highly of
gifted	very intelligent
height	how tall someone is
cluster	group together
infallible	always works correctly
whether	either
disentangle	separate
reared	raised
gap	difference
impulse	sudden idea
free flowing	not structured
hallmark	important quality
dimmer	not sharp
retrieve	recall, remember
stored	held in brain
grasp	understand
fuzzy	not clear
embodies	contains
mundane	common everyday experience or thing
water lily	type of plant that grows in ponds
hampered	held back
broader	applies to more settings
praise	kind words of approval

Thinking Critically

Evaluation

Which of the theories of intelligence best fits your notion of intelligence? Why?

Point/Counterpoint

Prepare an argument supporting each of the following positions:

a. Intelligence tests should be used in schools.
b. Intelligence tests should not be used in schools.

Psychology in Your Life

Give several examples of how tools of thinking (imagery and concepts) and problem-solving strategies (algorithms and heuristics) can be applied in your educational and personal life.

8

DEVELOPMENT

CHAPTER OUTLINE

This outline provides a way to organize your notes from both the text and the lecture. It will also serve as a review for the exam.

Module 8A Developmental Psychology: Basic Issues and Methodology	1. Controversial Issues in Developmental Psychology 2. Approaches to Studying Developmental Change

A Comparison of Longitudinal and Cross-Sectional Studies

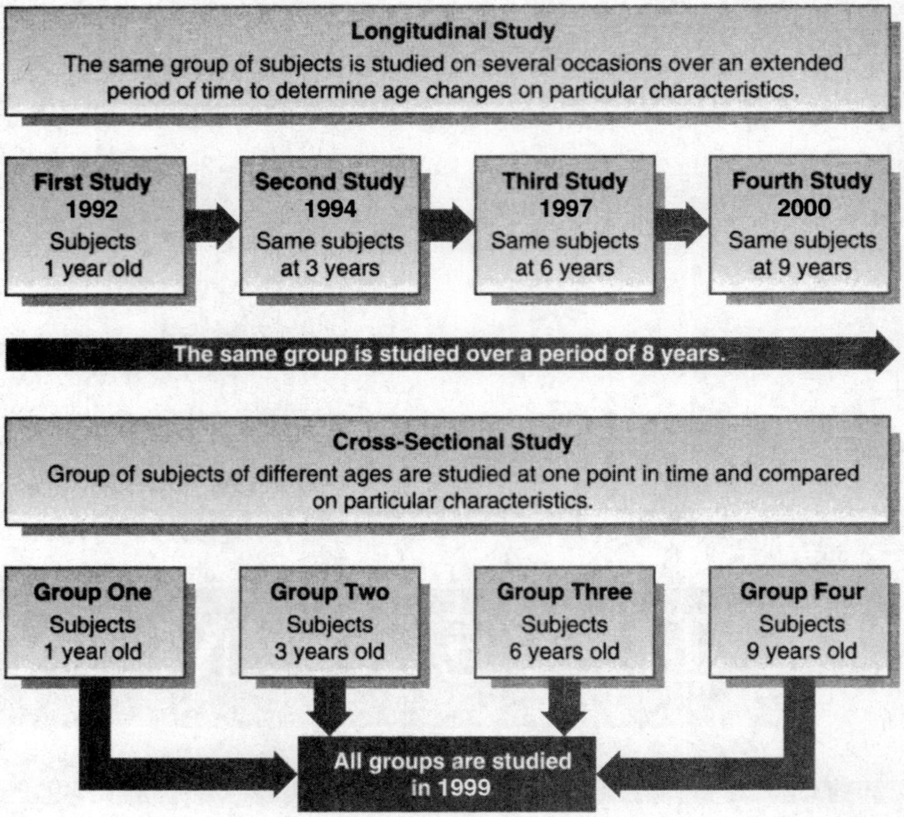

Module 8B Heredity and Prenatal Development

1. The Mechanism of Heredity: Genes and Chromosomes

   a. Dominant and Recessive Genes: Dominants Call the Shots

2. The Stages of Prenatal Development: Unfolding According to Plan

   a. Multiple Births: More Than One at a Time

      - Identical Twins (monozygotic)

      - Fraternal Twins (dizygotic)

3. Negative Influences on Prenatal Development: Sabotaging Nature's Plan

   - The Hazard of Drugs

   - Newborns at High Risk

Module 8C Physical Development and Learning

1. The Neonate

   - Reflexes: Built-In Responses

2. Perceptual Development in Infancy

   - Vision: What Newborns Can See

3. Learning in Infancy

4. Physical and Motor Development: Growing, Growing, Grown

   a. Infancy

   b. Puberty

   c. Middle Age

Module 8D The Cognitive Stages of Development: Climbing the Steps to Cognitive Maturity

1. Piaget's Stages of Cognitive Development

   a. The Sensorimotor Stage (Birth to Age Two)

   b. The Preoperational Stage (Ages Two to Seven)

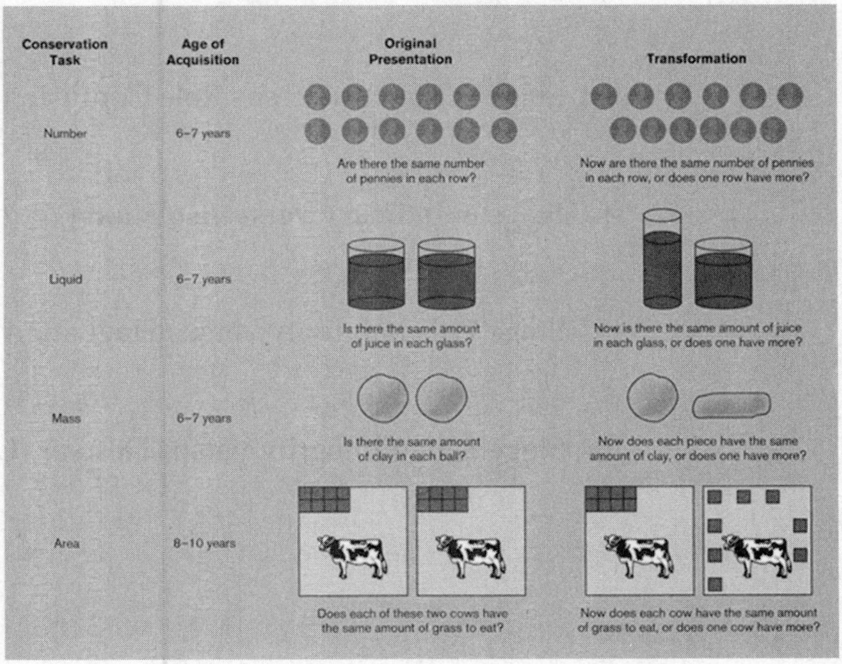

	c. The Concrete Operations Stage (Ages 7 to 11 or 12)
	d. The Formal Operations Stage (Ages 11 or 12 and Beyond)
	2. An Evaluation of Piaget's Contribution
	3. Intellectual Capacity During Adolescence, and Early, Middle, and Late Adulthood
Module 8E Socialization and Social Relationships	1. Erikson's Theory of Psychosocial Development • Psychosocial Stages a. Stage 1: Basic Trust versus Basic Mistrust (Birth to 12 Months) b. Stage 2: Autonomy versus Shame and Doubt (Ages One to Three) c. Stage 3: Initiative versus Guilt (Ages Three to Six) d. Stage 4: Industry versus Inferiority (Ages Six to Puberty) e. Stage 5: Identity versus Role Confusion (Adolescence) f. Stage 6: Intimacy versus Isolation (Young Adulthood) g. Stage 7: Generativity versus Stagnation (Middle Adulthood) h. Stage 8: Ego Integrity versus Despair (Late Adulthood)

2. The Parents' Role in the Socialization Process

a. Attachment in Infant Monkeys: Like Humans in So Many Ways

b. The Need for Love

c. The Development of Attachment in Humans

d. Ainsworth's Study of Attachment: The Importance of Being Securely Attached

i. Secure Attachment

ii. Avoidant Attachment

iii. Resistant Attachment

iv. Disorganized/Disoriented Attachment

v. Father-Child Attachment Relationships

e. Parenting Styles: What Works and What Doesn't

i. Authoritarian Parents

ii. Authoritative Parents

iii. Permissive Parents

	3. Socialization in Adolescence a. Adolescent Egocentrism: On Centre Stage, Unique, and Indestructible b. The Development of Physical Aggression 4. Kohlberg's Theory of Moral Development a. Levels of Moral Reasoning i. The Preconventional Level ii. The Conventional Level iii. The Postconventional Level b. The Development of Moral Reasoning c. Research on Kohlberg's Theory
Module 8F Special Concerns in Later Adulthood	1. Terminal Illness and Death a. Kübler-Ross on Death and Dying b. Bereavement
Apply It!	Choosing a Non-parental Care Arrangement.

Chapter Learning Objective Questions

Answer the following questions in the space provided and check your answers on the page numbers listed.

8.1 Identify three controversial issues in developmental psychology. p. 220	
8.2 Understand how each of the two opposing views in each of the controversial issues explain development. p. 220	
8.3 Compare and contrast the strengths and weaknesses of longitudinal and cross-sectional research designs. p. 220–221	
8.4 Explain how hereditary traits are transmitted. p. 221	
8.5 Define dominant and recessive genes and describe how they function. p. 222	
8.6 List the three stages of prenatal development and identify critical developments at each stage. p. 222–223	
8.7 Identify teratogens and explain their impact on development. p. 224	
8.8 Map out the key physical changes in development from infancy to middle age. p. 225–228	
8.9 Describe the sensory perceptual abilities of infants. p. 225	
8.10 Explain how neonates learn. p. 226	

8.11 Identify each of Piaget's stages. p. 228–230

8.12 Explain the key cognitive achievements for each of Piaget's stages. p. 228–230

8.13 Identify key changes in intellectual performance over the adult years. p. 231–233

8.14 Identify and describe each of Erikson's psychosocial stages. p. 233–235

8.15 Explain what Harlow's studies revealed about maternal deprivation and attachment in infant monkeys. p. 236

8.16 Describe the four types of attachment. p. 236–237

8.17 Understand how each of the three styles of parenting impacts on child development. p. 237

8.18 Define and describe adolescent egocentrism. p. 238

8.19 Identify and explain each of Kohlberg's three levels of moral reasoning. p. 239–240

8.20 Identify and describe the five stages Kubler-Ross proposed to explain the process of coming to terms with death and dying. p. 242

8.21 Understand the process of bereavement. p. 242

9.

Noti

Study Tips

Learn to study more effectively and improve your memory with these tips and practical exercises.

Effective Note-Taking During Class

1. **Review the textbook chapter before class.** Instructors often design a lecture based on the assumption that you have read the chapter before class. You can take notes more easily if you already have some idea of the material.
2. **Bring your favourite note-taking tools to class.** Make sure you have pencils, pens, highlighter markers, paper, note cards, or whatever materials you find useful.
3. **Sit as close to the instructor as possible.** You will have fewer distractions while taking your notes.
4. **Arrive at class early.** Relax and get your brain "tuned-up" to the subject by reviewing your notes from the previous class.
5. **Picture yourself up front with the instructor.** The more connected you feel to the material and the instructor, the more you will understand and remember the topic.
6. **Let go of judgments and debates.** Focus on understanding what the instructor is saying because that is what you will find on the test. Do not get distracted by evaluating the instructor's lecture style, appearance, or strange habits. When you hear something you disagree with, make a quick note of it and then let it go.
7. **Be active in class.** It is the best way to stay awake in class! Volunteer for demonstrations. Join in class discussions.

. **Relate the topic to an interest of yours.** We remember things that interest us.

Watch for clues of what is important.
   - repetition
   - summary statements
   - information written on the board
   - information the instructor takes directly from his or her notes

ce what interests the instructor.

Try It

Testing Child Development

Find a child who is between the ages of 3 and 5 and observe them trying the following tasks.

1. Locate three glasses, two the exact same shape and size, and the third one a noticeably different shape but able to hold about the same amount of liquid.

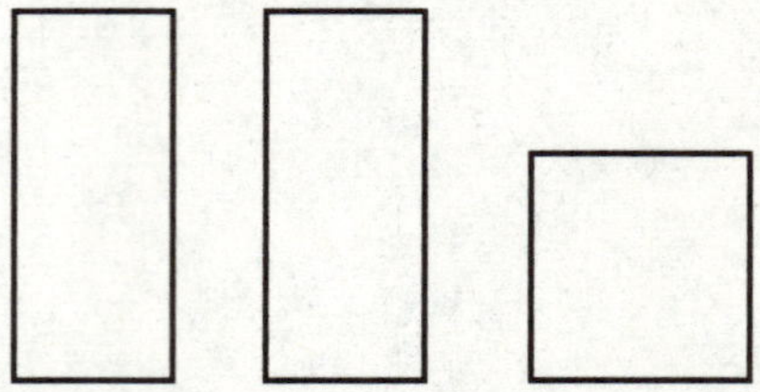

2. Fill the identical glasses with liquid up to the same level.
3. Ask the child which glass has more in it.
4. With the child watching, pour the liquid from one of the glasses into the glass of a different shape.
5. Ask the child which glass now has more in it.

What principle of Piaget have you demonstrated?

You can do further experiments by showing a child two balls of clay and then flattening one. Ask the child which ball of clay is bigger. You can also ask a child which sandwich is bigger, a half sandwich cut into three pieces or an uncut whole sandwich. (You must show the child the sandwiches.)

answer to Piaget question: conservation

Battle Procrastination

You might do fine when you study, but just to get to the books can be a challenge. How do you battle a common problem, procrastination? Some tips include the following:

1. Identify the environmental cues that habitually interfere with your studying.
2. Schedule your study time and reinforce yourself for adhering to your schedule.
3. Get started. Just open the book and get moving. That's the hard part.
4. Use visualization of negative consequences if you don't get the work done.
5. Become better at estimating how long it takes to complete an assignment.
6. Avoid jumping to another task when you reach the difficult part of an assignment.
7. Avoid preparation overkill. Don't plan for hours and then work for minutes

Practice Multiple-Choice Test

After studying the text and completing the Study Guide activities, answer these questions to determine if you need to review any areas before your exam.

1. Which of the following issues is most closely associated with the nature–nurture controversy?
   a. To what extent are personal characteristics stable over time?
   b. To what degree do heredity and environment influence development?
   c. Is it ethical to compare the development of humans and animals?
   d. Is development continuous or does it occur in stages?

2. A gene is said to be recessive when:
   a. it is covered by the other gene in the chromosome.
   b. its influence is obscured if it is paired with a dominant gene.
   c. it is smaller than the dominant gene.
   d. it does not appear in the individual's genotype.

3. Which of the following is not a stage of prenatal development?
   a. period of the fetus
   b. period of the zygote
   c. period of the ovum
   d. period of the embryo

4. What are some negative influences on prenatal development?
   a. certain prescription and nonprescription drugs
   b. poor maternal nutrition
   c. maternal infections and illnesses
   d. all of the above

5. A researcher who compares the level of education in groups of different ages to see the influence of education on successful aging is conducting a:
   a. genetic study
   b. longitudinal study
   c. difference study
   d. cross-sectional study

6. Pick the response that best describes the sensory ability of the newborn.
   a. Not all of the newborn's senses are functional at birth.
   b. The neonate has preferences for certain sounds.
   c. The neonate does not have taste preference yet.
   d. All of the above.

7. What type of learning occurs in the first few days of life?
   a. habituation
   b. classical conditioning
   c. operant conditioning and observational learning
   d. all of the above

8. All of the following are secondary sex characteristics EXCEPT:
   a. breast development in females.
   b. underarm and pubic hair in both sexes.
   c. ovaries in females.
   d. voice change in males.

9. Harlow's classic research with infant monkeys has illustrated the importance of which of the following in early development?
   a. contact comfort
   b. regular feeding
   c. freedom to explore
   d. a stimulating environment

10. What are the four attachment patterns?
    a. tight, loose, fragmented, solid
    b. reserved, fearful, schema, and conceptual
    c. secure, resistant, avoidant, and disorganized/disoriented
    d. dependent, independent, marginal, main

11. According to Piaget what is the major accomplishment of the sensorimotor stage?
    a. abstract thinking
    b. egocentrism
    c. centration
    d. object permanence

12. What cognitive limitation characterizes a child's thinking during the preoperational stage?
    a. egocentrism
    b. centration
    c. lack of conservation and reversibility
    d. all of the above

13. During the stage of concrete operations children:
    a. understand the concept of reversibility.
    b. do not yet understand the concept of conservation.
    c. are able to solve abstract problems.
    d. none of the above.

14. What new capability characterizes the formal operations stage?
    a. concrete thinking
    b. conservation
    c. reversibility
    d. abstract thinking

15. Which of the following statements would apply to an adult education class?
    a. Since all of the students will have obtained formal operational thought, relevance will be crucial.
    b. It is possible that many of these adults may not have attained the skills of formal operational thought.
    c. Probably fewer than 15 percent of the class can solve theoretical problems.
    d. none of the above

16. Adolescents who feel they are protected from misfortune are experiencing a
    a. personal fable
    b. cognitive impairment
    c. moral dilemma
    d. pretend audience

17. At Kohlberg's conventional level, the morality of a particular action is determined by whether or not the:
    a. actions help the individual to satisfy personal needs.
    b. individual's actions uphold self-chosen ethical standards.
    c. individual's actions will be approved by other persons.
    d. individual's actions result in punishment.

18. Carol Gilligan criticized Kohlberg for:
    a. concentrating too much on moral reasoning and too little on moral behaviour.
    b. claiming that his moral stages apply to people in all cultures.
    c. having underestimated the percentage of people who reach the postconventional level.
    d. having a theory that is sex-biased.

19. Erikson's theory emphasizes:
    a. a person's relationship to the social and cultural environment.
    b. the type of logic that underlies thought processes.
    c. life and its inherent rewards and punishments.
    d. active mental processes.

20. According to Baumrind what are three parenting styles?
    a. aristocratic, formal, and humanistic
    b. authoritarian, permissive, and authoritative
    c. formal, informal, and inconsistent
    d. easy, difficult, and slow-to-warm-up

21. How do peers contribute to the socialization process?
    a. modelling and reinforcing appropriate behaviours
    b. punishing inappropriate behaviour
    c. providing an objective measure for children to evaluate their own abilities
    d. all of the above

22. Erik Erikson would be most likely to say that one of the problems resulting from adolescent drug use is that it:
    a. interferes with the task of identity formation.
    b. fosters a sense of guilt and inferiority.
    c. is a threat to health and safety.
    d. is an early symptom of emotional disorders.

23. In late adulthood, regular exercise:
    a. is not desirable.
    b. can greatly increase energy and fitness.
    c. increases the risk of heart attack.
    d. is not as important as at earlier ages.

24. Which of the following is the correct sequence of Kübler-Ross's stages of dying?
    a. denial, depression, anger, bargaining, acceptance
    b. depression, denial, anger, bargaining, acceptance
    c. anger, denial, bargaining, depression, acceptance
    d. denial, anger, bargaining, depression, acceptance

25. The infant's vision at birth is about 20/600 and does not reach an adult level until about age ______.
    a. 6 months
    b. 12 months
    c. 18 months
    d. 2 years

Answers to Multiple-Choice Questions

Question Number	Answer	Explanation for application questions
1.	b.	
2.	b.	A recessive gene is expressed when it is paired with another recessive gene.
3.	c.	
4.	d.	All of the responses are true.
5.	d.	
6.	b.	All of the newborn's senses are functional at birth.
7.	d.	All of the responses are true.
8.	c.	
9.	a.	
10.	c.	
11.	d.	Object permanence is the major accomplishment of this stage.
12.	d.	All responses are correct.
13.	a.	Children at the concrete operations stage become able to decentre their thinking and to understand the concepts of reversibility and conservation.
14.	d.	Abstract problem solving is the most significant cognitive development.
15.	b.	Not everyone reaches the formal operations stage.
16.	a.	
17.	c.	
18.	d.	
19.	a.	Erikson's stages are called psychosocial and emphasize our relationship to society.
20.	b.	
21.	d.	All responses are correct.
22.	a.	
23.	b.	
24.	d.	
25.	d.	

Glossary for Text Language Enhancement

Students identified the following words from the text as needing more explanation. This page can be cut out, folded in half, and used as a bookmark for this chapter.

term	definition
lush	many plants
squeal	high-pitched sound
edible	can be eaten
squat	sit on the back of legs
slaughtered	killed
lifespan	through one's life
eras	periods of time
transmission	act of passing on characteristics by heredity
Genome	study chromosomes
gene pool	the possible genetic combinations available in a particular place
stillbirth	baby born dead
stroke	pet
fixate	stare
milestones	significant events
culminates	ends
comprehensive	detailed
systematically	done in steps
egocentrism	thinking of the world only from your own point of view
inanimate	without life
obstacles	things that block your way
monumental	important
conventional wisdom	commonly accepted belief
downhill	a state of decline
expertise	special skill or knowledge
mistrust	not trusting
resolution	completion, to finish
mischief	bad behaviour
bonding	mutual connection
stare fixedly	look without moving
mesh	wire fencing
crib	bed for babies
draped	covered
stare	look
dwarfism	very small size
gazes	looks
peer group	people the same age as you
delinquency	adolescent illegal activity

term	definition
impulsive	acts quickly without thinking
indestructibility	cannot be destroyed
dilemmas	problems with several answers possible, difficult to pick one
contemplate	think about
inconsolably	not to be comforted

Thinking Critically

Evaluation

In your opinion, do Erikson's psychosocial stages for adolescence and early adulthood accurately represent the major conflicts of these periods of life? Explain.

Point/Counterpoint

Prepare an argument supporting each of these positions:

a. Physical development peaks in the early adult years and declines thereafter.

b. Physical development can be maintained throughout life.

Psychology in Your Life

Using Erikson's theory, try to relate the first four stages of psychosocial development to your life.

Using Baumrind's scheme, classify the parenting style your mother and/or father used in rearing you.

a. Cite examples of techniques they used that support your classification.

b. Do you agree with Baumrind's conclusions about the effects of that parenting style on children? Explain.

9

MOTIVATION AND EMOTION

CHAPTER OUTLINE

This outline provides a way to organize your notes from both the text and the lecture. It will also serve as a review for the exam.

Module 9A Theories of Motivation

1. Instinct Theories of Motivation

2. Drive-Reduction Theory: Striving to Keep a Balanced Internal State

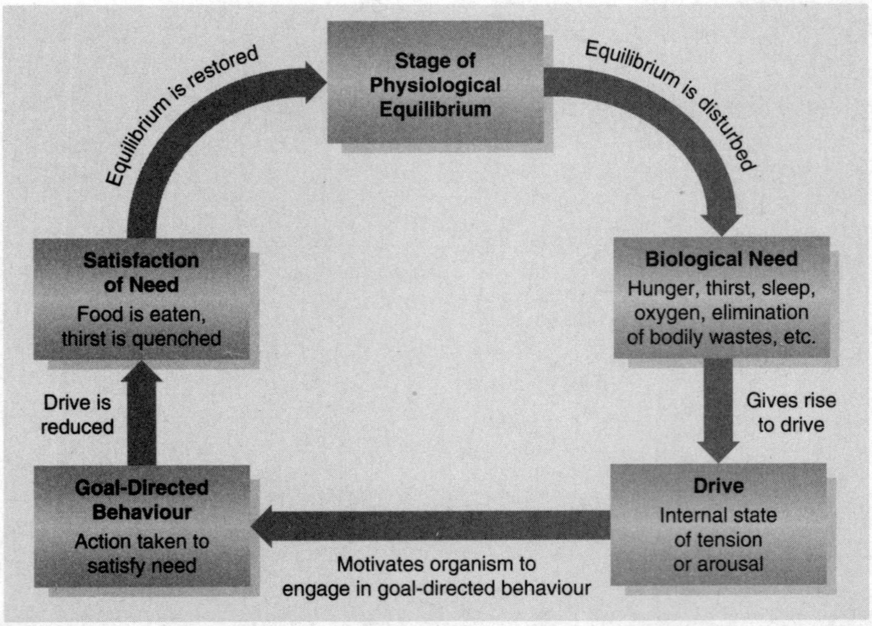

3. Arousal Theory: Striving for an Optimal Level of Arousal

   a. Stimulus Motives: Increasing Stimulation

   b. Arousal and Performance

   c. The Effects of Sensory Deprivation: Sensory Nothingness

4. Maslow's Hierarchy of Needs: Putting Our Needs in Order

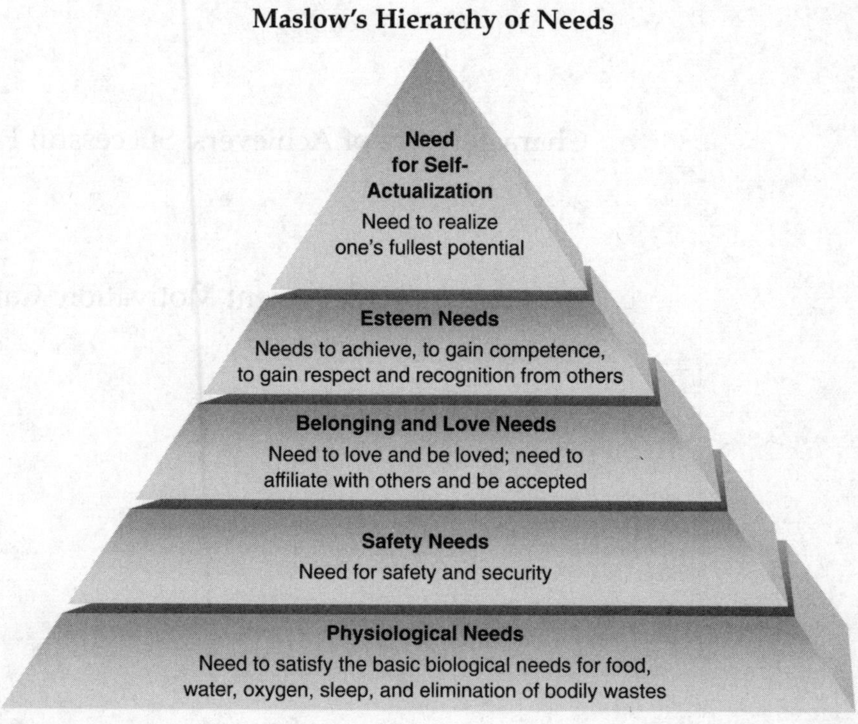

Module 9B The Primary Drives: Hunger and Thirst	1. Thirst: We All Have Two Kinds 2. The Biological Basis of Hunger: Internal Hunger Cues 3. Other Factors Influencing Hunger: External Eating Cues 4. Understanding Variations in Body Weight: Why We Weigh What We Weigh
Module 9C Social Motives	1. The Need for Achievement: The Drive to Excel a. Atkinson's Theory of Achievement Motivation: When Do We Try? b. Characteristics of Achievers: Successful People Have Them c. Developing Achievement Motivation: Can We Learn It?

Module 9D The What and Why of Emotions	1. Motivation and Emotion: What Is the Connection? 2. The Components of Emotions: The Physical, the Cognitive, and the Behavioural 3. Theories of Emotion: Which Comes First, the Thought or the Feeling? a. The James-Lange Theory b. The Cannon-Bard Theory c. The Schachter-Singer theory d. The Lazarus Cognitive-Appraisal Theory
Module 9E The Expression of Emotions	1. The Range of Emotion: How Wide Is It? 2. The Development of Facial Expressions in Infants: Smiles and Frowns Come Naturally 3. Cultural Rules for Displaying Emotion 4. Emotion as a Form of Communication

Module 9F Experiencing Emotion	1. The Facial-Feedback Hypothesis: Does the Face Cause the Feeling? 2. Emotion and Rational Thinking 3. Love: The Strongest Emotional Bond
Apply It!	Eating Disorders: The Tyranny of the Scale

Chapter Learning Objective Questions

Answer the following questions in the space provided and check your answers on the page numbers listed.

9.1 Compare and contrast internal and external motivation. p. 250	
9.2 Identify and contrast the four main theories of motivation described in the chapter, including instinct theories, drive-reduction theory, arousal theory, and Maslow's hierarchy of needs. p. 250–253	
9.3 Explain how stimulus motives and arousal affect behaviour and performance. p. 252	
9.4 Describe the effects of sensory deprivation. p. 252	
9.5 Describe Maslow's hierarchy of needs and explain how it connects to motivation. p. 253	
9.6 Describe and compare the two kinds of thirst. p. 254–255	
9.7 Explain the role of the lateral and ventromedial hypothalamus in moderating hunger. p. 255	
9.8 Describe the biologically driven internal hunger cues. p. 255	
9.9 Describe the various types of external cues that influence hunger and explain how they function. p. 257	

9.10 Describe how social and genetic factors contribute to weight. p. 257	
9.11 Describe and contrast the fat-cell and set-point theories and contrast their main arguments. p. 257–258	
9.12 Describe social motives and explain how they relate to motivation. p. 258	
9.13 Explain how the need for achievement influences expectations and performance. p. 258–259	
9.14 Describe the various characteristics of achievers. p. 259	
9.15 Explain the connection between motivation and emotion. p. 261	
9.16 Describe and contrast the physical, cognitive, and behavioural components of emotions and contrast how these components affect emotions. p. 261	
9.17 Compare and contrast the four theories of emotion described in the chapter: James-Lange theory, Cannon-Bard theory, Schachter Singer theory, and Lazarus theory. p. 262–263	
9.18 Identify the basic emotions. p. 264	

9.19 Describe the developmental process associated with emotional expression. p. 264

9.20 Describe display rules and explain how context and culture affect them. p. 265

9.21 Explain how emotions can serve as a form of communication. p. 265

9.22 Explain the facial-feedback hypothesis. p. 267

9.23 Describe how facial expressions can affect emotions. p. 267

9.24 Compare and contrast passionate and companionate love. p. 269

9.25 Describe the six styles of love identified by John Allan Lee. p. 269

9.26 Describe Sternberg's triarchic theory of love and explain the various kinds of love that can emerge as a result of these components. p. 269

Study Tips Try It

Learn to study more effectively and improve your memory with these tips and practical exercises.

When Instructors Talk Too Fast

1. Read the material before class.
2. Review notes with classmates.
3. Leave large empty spaces in your notes.
4. Have a symbol that indicates to you that you have missed something.
5. Write down key points only and revise your notes right after class to add details.
6. Choose to focus on what you believe to be key information.
7. See the instructor after class and fill in what you missed.
8. Ask the instructor to slow down if you think that is appropriate.

Staying With It

We have all experienced daydreaming or the voices in our mind that are busy judging and evaluating everything around us. These activities interfere without focusing on what we are trying to learn at the moment.

The following are ideas you can try the next time your mind takes time out:

1. Notice that your mind has wandered.
2. Don't fight it because the thought will just fight back.
3. Gently bring your mind back to the room.
4. Notice how your chair feels, what temperature the room is, and any smells in the room.
5. Practise noticing and letting go of your inner voices. It gets much easier with practice.
6. Your inner voices are helpful when you need to be creative or analytical. With practice you can quiet the voices when you are taking in new information and put the voices to good work when you are reviewing and organizing your notes.

Improving Memory with Mnemonic Devices

Mnemonics are memory aids that have been developed to help us remember things. They include:

1. **Rhyme**—Organizing material so that it rhymes helps you to remember and ensures all of the material will be recalled in order.

2. **First-Letter Technique**—Arrange the first letters of each word into a list you need to remember. Form meaningful chunks out of the first letters, or use them to create a saying or phrase (e.g., Roy G. Biv for the colour spectrum, or Every Good Boy Deserves Fudge for the lines of the treble clef.

3. **Method of Loci**—If something needs to be recalled in a specific order, it may help to visualize the items in a location you are familiar with (e.g., your home).

4. **Keyword Method**—Imagining the new word you are trying to remember in an unusually vivid and bizarre manner may help you recall the information.

Practice Multiple-Choice Test

After studying the text and completing the Study Guide activities, answer these questions to determine if you need to review any areas before your exam.

1. Motivation is defined as a process that:
   a. initiates, directs, and sustains behaviour.
   b. changes behaviour as a result of prior experience.
   c. reflects physical and behavioural attempts to cope and adapt.
   d. is a relatively stable personality tendency.

2. Which of the following best describes extrinsic motivation?
   a. the desire to engage in an activity simply because it is enjoyable
   b. the desire to perform an act to gain a reward or to avoid an undesirable consequence
   c. the desire to perform an act that is part of instinctive behaviour
   d. working very hard to learn the principles of psychology because you find it interesting

3. An inborn, unlearned, fixed action pattern of behaviour that is characteristic of an entire species is referred to as:
   a. an emotion.
   b. an achievement motive.
   c. an instinct.
   d. an affiliation motive.

4. Drive-reduction theory assumes that various motives like hunger and thirst have in common the fact that they:
   a. are aroused by external stimuli.
   b. are unpleasant sensations we want to reduce or eliminate.
   c. cause us to behave in ways that increase our need level.
   d. are learned reactions.

5. The body's natural tendency to maintain a state of internal balance or equilibrium is referred to as:
   a. arousal.
   b. opponent process.
   c. homeostasis.
   d. instinct.

6. Which of the following theories suggests that the aim of motivation is to maintain an optimal level of arousal?
   a. attribution theory
   b. arousal theory
   c. drive-reduction theory
   d. instinct theory

7. According to the text, some researchers claim that emotional feelings are negative when people are:
   a. underaroused.
   b. overaroused.
   c. either underaroused or overaroused.
   d. at optimal arousal.

8. Which of the following suggests that performance on tasks is best when arousal levels are appropriate to the difficulty of the risk?
   a. instinctual theory of motivation
   b. James-Lange theory
   c. Maslow's hierarchy of needs
   d. the Yerkes-Dodson law

9. Which of the following conditions is not associated with prolonged sensory deprivation?
   a. inability to concentrate
   b. a satisfying, relaxed feeling
   c. hallucinations
   d. confusion

10. According to Maslow's hierarchy of needs, which of the following would need to be satisfied before a person would try to satisfy belonging and love needs?
    a. safety and self-actualization needs
    b. self-actualization and esteem needs
    c. physiological and safety needs
    d. physiological and esteem needs

11. One type of thirst develops from a loss of bodily fluid, which can be caused by all of the following except:
    a. perspiring.
    b. vomiting.
    c. excessive intake of alcohol.
    d. excessive intake of salt.

12. Which of the following is one of the body's satiety signals?
    a. high blood levels of glucose
    b. low blood levels of glucose
    c. high insulin levels
    d. stomach contractions

13. What hormone helps the body convert glucose to energy?
    a. the gastrointestinal hormone
    b. insulin
    c. CCK
    d. acetylcholine

14. The theory that suggests humans and other mammals are genetically programmed to maintain a certain amount of body weight is known as the:
a. metabolic set theory.
b. set-point theory.
c. fat-cell theory.
d. insulin utilization curve.

15. After trying many diets, losing and regaining weight repeatedly, a person can reach a point where the body gains weight quickly and loses it slowly. This phenomena of weight cycling is also called:
a. set-point weight.
b. fat-cell thermostat.
c. yo-yo dieting.
d. fat-cell theory.

16. How quickly your body burns calories to produce energy depends on your:
a. set-point.
b. metabolic rate.
c. fat cells.
d. food intake.

17. Increased exercise during dieting is important to counteract the body's tendency to:
a. increase the fat in the fat cells.
b. increase the number of fat cells.
c. lower its metabolic rate.
d. raise its metabolic rate.

18. The Thematic Apperception Text (TAT) involves showing subjects a series of ambiguous pictures and asking them to:
a. remember them.
b. write stories about them.
c. reproduce them.
d. correctly identify and label what each depicts.

19. Concerns with meeting standards of excellence and accomplishing difficult tasks refers to the:
a. need for affiliation.
b. need for achievement.
c. need for power.
d. need for apperception.

20. Individuals who are high in achievement motivation tend to:
a. avoid opportunities for constructive feedback.
b. prefer situations involving moderate levels of risk or difficulty.
c. avoid opportunities that meet only moderate goals.
d. prefer situations with very high task levels of risk or difficulty.

21. The three components of emotions are:
a. stimulus, arousal, and release.
b. arousal, loss of control, and regaining control.
c. behaviour, physiological, and cognitive.
d. motor, sensory, and cognitive.

22. The theory that emotional feelings result when we become aware of our physiological response to an emotion-provoking stimulus is the:
a. Cannon-Bard theory.
b. James-Lange theory.
c. Schachter-Singer theory.
d. facial feedback theory.

23. According to which of the following theories of emotion do the subjective reactions we label as fear and anxiety appear simultaneously with the physiological changes that accompany the emotion?
a. Schachter-Singer theory
b. Cannon-Bard theory
c. James-Lange theory
d. instinct theory

24. Some investigators have examined the facial expressions of subjects experiencing various basic emotions. When researchers compared the facial expressions of persons from different parts of the world, they found:
a. little similarity in facial expressions across cultures.
b. very similar facial expressions across cultures.
c. extreme variations in most of the basic emotions.
d. that few people are able to recognize these facial expressions.

25. The cultural rules that dictate how emotions should be expressed and where it is appropriate to express them are called:
a. facial-feedback hypotheses.
b. stimulus motives.
c. display rules.
d. gesture systems.

26. When subjects are instructed to exaggerate their facial expressions while viewing emotion-producing stimuli, it has been found that they:
a. no longer report an emotional reaction to the stimuli.
b. report a less intense emotional reaction to the stimuli.
c. report an intensified emotional reaction to the stimuli.
d. often report an emotional reaction that is opposite to the normally experienced emotion.

Answers to Multiple Choice Questions

Question Number	Answer	Explanation for application questions
1.	a.	
2.	b.	Extrinsic motivation is rewards and punishments.
3.	c.	
4.	b.	
5.	c.	
6.	b.	
7.	c.	
8.	d.	
9.	b.	
10.	c.	
11.	d.	One reason for thirst is loss of fluids due to perspiration, vomiting, or intake of alcohol.
12.	a.	
13.	b.	
14.	b.	
15.	c.	
16.	b.	
17.	c.	Exercise is able to counteract the body's natural tendency to decrease the metabolic rate when calories are reduced.
18.	b.	
19.	b.	
20.	b.	
21.	c.	
22.	b.	James-Lange's theory states that emotional feelings result from awareness of our physiological state.
23.	a.	
24.	b.	
25.	c.	
26.	c.	

Glossary for Text Language Enhancement

Students identified the following words from the text as needing more explanation. This page can be cut out, folded in half, and used as a bookmark for this chapter.

term	definition
aspirations	what we hope to become
initiate	start
sustain	support
arousal	increased tension
sluggish	slow
chamber	small room
intricate	complex
invariant	not changing
dehydrated	took water out of
satiety	the feeling of having had more than one wants
obese	extremely overweight
distended	expanded
elevations	increases
mutated	changed
vigorously	with great effort
drawn to	attracted to
ambiguous	having no specific meaning; unclear
attain	gain, achieve
strive	try
peg	short stick
burglar	someone who steals things
frenzy	very nervous state
emerge	to come forth
stony-faced	show no emotion on your face
subtle	faint
swept away	overpowered by
eating binges	eating large amounts of food
purge	get rid of the food
gorge	to stuff oneself with food
triggers	starts

Thinking Critically

Evaluation

In your view, which theory or combination of theories best explains motivation: drive-reduction theory, arousal theory, or Maslow's hierarchy of needs? Which theory do you find least convincing? Support your answers.

Using what you have learned about body weight and dieting, select any well-known weight-loss plan (for example, Weight Watchers, Jenny Craig, Slim-Fast) and evaluate it, explaining why it is or is not an effective way to lose weight and keep it off.

Point/Counterpoint

Recent research suggests that individuals who work in the prevention of crime, such as police officers, airport security, and border officials, should be trained to read people's emotions since it is difficult to fake a true emotion. Prepare a convincing argument supporting each of the following positions:

a. Training security personnel to read facial expressions accurately should not be allowed.
b. Training security personnel to read facial expressions accurately should be allowed.

Psychology in Your Life

Which level of Maslow's hierarchy (shown in Figure 9.2) provides the strongest motivation for your behaviour in general? Give specific examples to support your answer.

10

SOCIAL PSYCHOLOGY

CHAPTER OUTLINE

This outline provides a way to organize your notes from both the text and the lecture. It will also serve as a review for the exam.

Module 10A Social Perception	1. Impression Formation: Sizing Up the Other Person 2. Attribution: Our Explanation of Behaviour
Module 10B Attraction	1. Factors Influencing Attraction a. Proximity: Close to You b. Reciprocal Liking: Liking Those Who Like Us c. Attractiveness: Good Looks Attract d. Similarity: A Strong Basis of Attraction

2. Romantic Attraction

3. Mate Selection: The Mating Game

Module 10C Conformity, Obedience, and Compliance

1. Conformity: Going Along with the Group
   - Asch's Experiment: The Classic on Conformity
2. Obedience: Following Orders
   - The Milgram Study: The Classic on Obedience
   - Variations of the Milgram Study
3. Compliance: Giving In to Requests
   - The Foot-in-the-Door Technique: Upping the Ante
   - The Door-in-the-Face Technique: An Unreasonable Request First
   - The Low-Ball Technique: Not Telling the Whole Truth Up Front
   - Other Techniques: Wording of Requests and Increasing Guilt

---

Module 10D Group Influence

1. The Effects of the Group on Individual Performance

   a. Social Facilitation: Performing in the Presence of Others

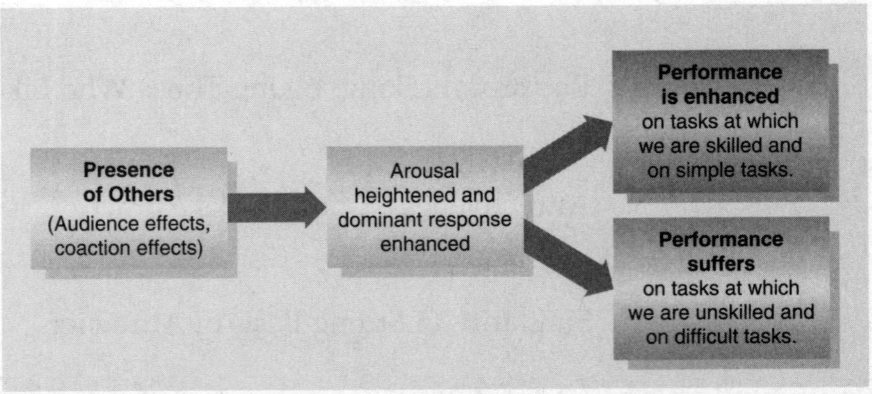

b. Social Loafing: Not Pulling Our Weight in a Group Effort

2. The Effects of the Group on Decision Making

   a. Group Polarization: When Group Decisions Become More Extreme

   b. Groupthink: When Group Cohesiveness Leads to Bad Decisions

3. Social Roles

   • Zimbardo's Prison Study: Our Roles Dictate Our Actions

Module 10E Attitudes and Attitude Change

1. Attitudes: Cognitive, Emotional, and Behavioural Positions

   a. The Relationship between Attitudes and Behaviour

The Three Components of an Attitude

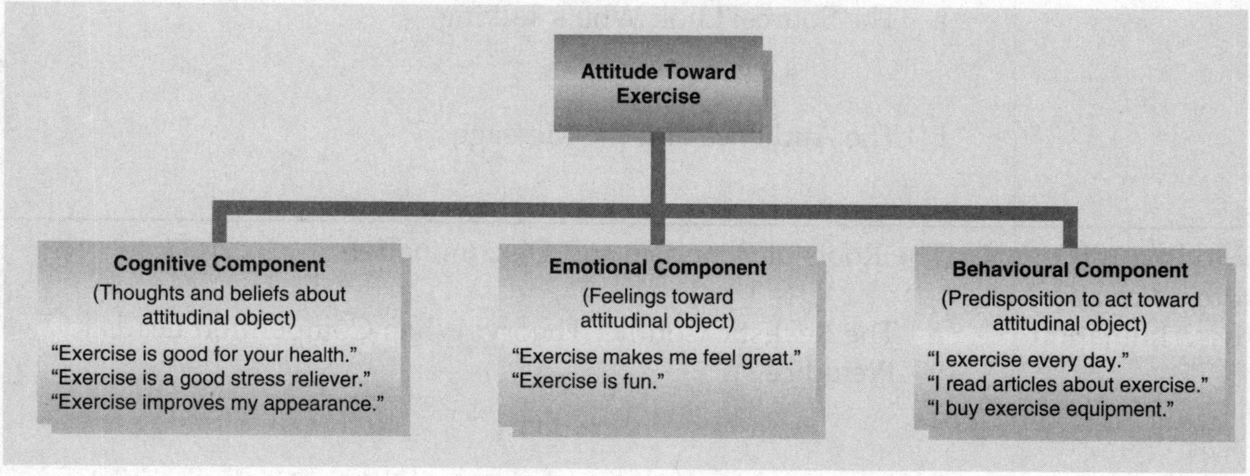

b. Cognitive Dissonance: The Mental Pain of Inconsistency

Methods of Reducing Cognitive Dissonance

Cognitive dissonance can occur when people become aware of inconsistencies in their attitudes or between their attitudes and their behaviour. People try to reduce dissonance by (1) changing their behaviour, (2) changing their attitude, (3) explaining away the inconsistency, or (4) reducing its importance. Here are examples of how a smoker might use these methods to reduce the cognitive dissonance created by his or her habit.

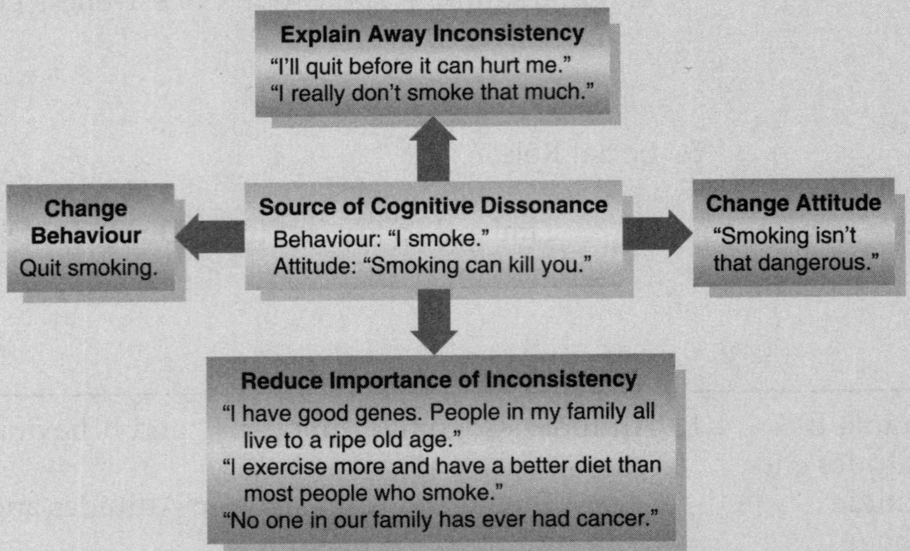

2. Persuasion: Trying to Change Attitudes

a. The Source: Look Who's Talking

b. The Audience and the Message

Module 10F Prejudice and Discrimination

1. The Roots of Prejudice and Discrimination

a. The Realistic Conflict Theory: When Competition Leads to Prejudice

b. Us versus Them: Dividing the World into In-Groups and Out-Groups

c. The Social Learning Theory: Acquiring Prejudice through Modelling and Reinforcement

d. Social Cognition: Natural Thinking Processes Can Lead to Prejudice

e. Reverse Discrimination: Bending Over Backward To Be Fair

2. Combating Prejudice and Discrimination

a. Direct Contact: Bringing Diverse Groups Together

b. Us versus Them: Extending the Boundaries of Narrowly Defined Social Groups

3. Prejudice: Is It Increasing or Decreasing?

Module 10G Prosocial Behaviour: Behaviour That Benefits Others

1. The Bystander Effect: The Greater the Number of Bystanders, the Less Likely They Are to Help

The Bystander Effect

In their intercom experiment, Darley and Latané showed that the more people a participant believed were present during an emergency, the longer it took that participant to respond and help a person in distress. (Data from Darley and Latané 1968a.)

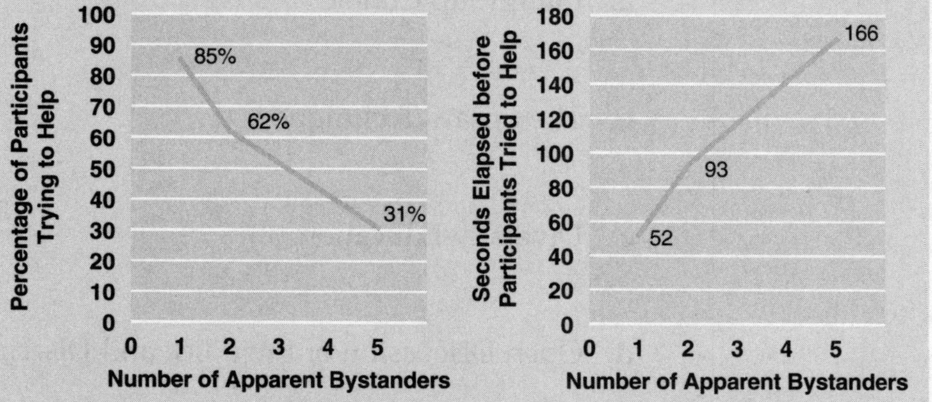

	2. People Who Help in Emergencies
Module 10H Aggression: Intentionally Harming Others	1. Biological versus Social Factors in Aggression 2. Aggression in Response to Frustration: Sometimes, But Not Always Frustration–Aggression Hypothesis Scapegoating 3. Aggression in Response to Aversive Events: Pain, Heat, Noise, and More 4. The Social Learning Theory of Aggression: Learning to Be Aggressive a. The Media and Aggression: Is There a Connection?
Apply It!	"Unlearning" Prejudice a. Intergroup Contact b. The Jigsaw Technique c. Diversity Education d. Open Discussion of Prejudice and Discrimination

Chapter Learning Objective Questions

Answer the following questions in the space provided and check your answers on the page numbers listed.

10.1 Describe the primacy effect. p. 278	
10.2 Explain how our expectations of people can become self-fulfilling prophecies. p. 278	
10.3 Describe and contrast situational and dispositional attributions. p. 278	
10.4 Identify three attribution biases when we explain our own vs. other people's behaviour. p. 279	
10.5 Describe the influence of proximity, reciprocal liking, and similarity on attraction. p. 280–281	
10.6 Explain the halo effect. p. 281	
10.7 Explain the matching hypothesis. p. 281	
10.8 Identify four qualities both men and women across cultures look for in a mate. p. 282	
10.9 Describe and compare conformity and compliance. p. 285	
10.10 Explain the finding of Asch's experiment on conformity. p. 285	

10.11 Explain the findings of Milgram's experiment on obedience. p. 285

10.12 Describe three techniques used to gain compliance. p. 286

10.13 Describe social facilitation. p. 286

10.14 Explain the influence of audience effects and co-action effects on individual performance. p. 286–287

10.15 Identify factors that can lessen social loafing. p. 287

10.16 Explain group polarization and why it does not affect all group decisions. p. 288

10.17 Describe social roles. p. 288

10.18 Identify the three components of an attitude. p. 289

10.19 Describe ways that individuals try to reduce cognitive dissonance. p. 290

10.20 Identify four elements of persuasion. p. 290–291

10.21 Describe the influence of credibility, attractiveness, and likeability on persuasion. p. 291	
10.22 Describe when fear-based appeals are most effective in persuading an audience. p. 291	
10.23 Describe the difference between prejudice and discrimination. p. 292–293	
10.24 Describe the effects of in-group and out-group categorizations and their role in discrimination. p. 293	
10.25 Explain prejudice according to social learning theory. p. 293	
10.26 Explain when the contact hypothesis will work to reduce prejudice. p. 294–295	
10.27 Describe when the bystander effect is most likely to occur. p. 297	
10.28 Provide two possible explanations for the bystander effect. p. 297–298	
10.29 Describe altruism. p. 298	

10.30 Identify people who are more likely to receive help in an emergency. p. 298

10.31 Identify biological and social factors that can contribute to aggression. p. 299

10.32 Explain the frustration-aggression hypothesis. p. 299

10.33 Describe the practice of scapegoating. p. 299

10.34 Identify aversive events that have been related to aggression. p. 299

10.35 Explain aggression according to social learning theory. p. 300

Practice Multiple-Choice Test

After studying the text and completing the Study Guide activities, answer these questions to determine if you need to review any areas before your exam.

1. Which of the following areas of psychology focuses on the influences other people have on our thoughts, feelings, and behaviours?
   a. personality psychology
   b. social psychology
   c. developmental psychology
   d. clinical psychology

2. Which of the following statements is true of first impressions?
   a. They act as filters for later information.
   b. They cannot be changed.
   c. They are usually correct.
   d. They are not particularly important.

3. When our expectations of another influence how the other person acts, the result is:
   a. a self-fulfilling prophecy.
   b. called the primary effect.
   c. referred to as the fundamental attribution error.
   d. a self-serving bias.

4. Attribution deals with the question of:
   a. why we and others act the way we do.
   b. how we can best achieve our goals.
   c. what the consequences of our actions will be.
   d. who our best choices for friends are.

5. The tendency of people to overemphasize dispositional causes and underemphasize situational causes when they explain the behaviour of others is called:
   a. the fundamental attributions.
   b. dispositional attributions.
   c. internal attributions.
   d. unbiased attributions.

6. Self-serving bias refers to our tendency to use:
   a. situational attributions for our behaviour.
   b. internal attributions for our behaviour.
   c. internal attributions for our successes and external attributions for our failures.
   d. internal attributions for our failures and external attributions for our successes.

7. The term that refers to the fact that interpersonal attraction is influenced by the physical closeness of other people to us:
   a. cognitive dissonance.
   b. ingratiation.
   c. proximity.
   d. priming.

8. Which of the following is best supported by research on interpersonal attraction?
   a. Familiarity breeds contempt.
   b. Absence makes the heart grow fonder.
   c. Opposites attract.
   d. Similarities attract.

9. When a person changes attitudes or behaviour to be consistent with the attitudes and behaviour of other people or with social norms, which of the following has occurred?
   a. conformity
   b. obedience
   c. deindividuation
   d. social facilitation

10. What is the term for a strategy used to gain first a favourable response to a small request, with the intent of making a person more likely to agree later to a larger request?
    a. planting-the-seed technique
    b. door-in-the-face technique
    c. foot-in-the-door technique
    d. that's-not-all-folks technique

11. The term social facilitation refers to:
    a. positive effects on one's performance due to the presence of others.
    b. negative effects on one's performance due to the presence of others.
    c. both positive and negative effects on one's performance due to the presence of others.
    d. negative effects on performance due to the absence of others.

12. Social loafing is most likely to occur when:
    a. individual output is monitored.
    b. individual output is evaluated.
    c. a task is challenging.
    d. individual output cannot be identified.

13. When group polarization occurs following group discussion, the group will decide to take a greater risk if they:
    a. were leaning in a cautious direction to begin with.
    b. were leaning in a risky direction to begin with.
    c. were leaning in different directions to begin with.
    d. regardless of the initial position of the group.

14. The three components of an attitude are:
    a. positive, negative, and neutral effect.
    b. the source, the message, and the medium.
    c. the cognitive, the emotional, and the behavioural.
    d. the opinion, the belief, and the knowledge.

15. Research on attitudes suggests that an attitude has all EXCEPT which of the following components?
    a. an emotional component
    b. a biochemical component
    c. a cognitive component
    d. a behavioural component

16. Which of the following would create the most cognitive dissonance?
    a. I bought a Toyota Corolla. I wish I had a Lexus.
    b. I like Italians. I don't like Italian food.
    c. I am an honest person. I cheated on the test.
    d. I should have gotten the job. I was not hired.

17. All of the following are components of persuasion except:
    a. the source.
    b. the framework.
    c. the message.
    d. the medium.

18. Prejudice is to __________ as discrimination is to __________.
    a. stereotypes; conflict
    b. attitudes; behaviours
    c. thought; competition
    d. in-group; out-group

19. According to the realistic conflict theory, prejudice develops because:
    a. realistic trait differences among ethnic groups are devalued rather than appreciated.
    b. human genes are programmed to compete with persons to whom we are not biologically related.
    c. of competition over scarce resources.
    d. individuals model the prejudice exhibited by family and friends.

20. Which of the following is an example of behaviour arising from us-versus-them social categories?
    a. helping a friend
    b. developing a sense of identity with your college because of its winning basketball team
    c. feeling insecure in an advanced psychology class you have chosen to take as an elective
    d. getting angry at the driver in the car in front of you

21. In the Robber's cave experiment, hostility and rivalry between two groups of boys was turned into cooperation by:
    a. having the two groups do pleasant activities together.
    b. having a crisis that requires both groups to work together.
    c. having an educational lecture on the value of cooperation.
    d. arranging for the two groups to have frequent contact with each other.

22. Recent research indicating that social cognition may play a role in the formation of prejudice and discrimination suggests that prejudice may spring from:
    a. our own natural thinking processes.
    b. in-group, out-group conflicts.
    c. competition among competing social groups.
    d. the realistic conflict theory.

23. The tendency to attribute generally positive or negative traits to a person as a result of observing one major positive or negative trait is called the:
   a. halo effect.
   b. exposure effect.
   c. group think.
   d. positive attribution theory.

24. According to social learning theory, attitudes of prejudice and hatred are learned by watching and mimicking:
   a. parents.
   b. teachers.
   c. peers.
   d. all of the above.

25. __________ is the tendency of members of a group, after group discussion, to shift toward a more extreme position in whatever direction they were leaning initially.
   a. Group polarization
   b. Groupthink
   c. Group role conversion
   d. Bolting

Answers to Multiple-Choice Questions

Question Number	Answer	Explanation for application questions
1.	b.	
2.	a.	
3.	a.	
4.	a.	
5.	a.	
6.	c.	
7.	c.	
8.	d.	
9.	a.	
10.	c.	
11.	c.	
12.	d.	
13.	a.	
14.	c.	
15.	b.	
16.	c.	
17.	b.	
18.	b.	
19.	c.	
20.	b.	
21.	b.	
22.	a.	
23	a.	
24.	d.	Children copy the behaviour t hey see including prejudice and hatred toward different racial, ethnic, or cultural groups.
25.	a.	

Glossary for Text Language Enhancement

Students identified the following words from the text as needing more explanation. This page can be cut out, folded in half, and used as a bookmark for this chapter.

term	definition
composition	made up of
francophones	people who speak French
anglophones	people who speak English
vacuum	without outside influence
provocative	exciting or arousing
atrocious	extremely cruel
shallow	without much thought
overemphasize	magnify, focus on too much
underemphasize	focus on too little
exposure	to have experience with
socioeconomic	social class and financial level
conform	go along with
norm	what is typical
confederates	people helping the experimenter
unanimous	unified, going together
stunned	shocked, very surprised
atrocities	very terrible acts
strapped	held in by belts
hasten	hurry
flip	press up or down
frantic	in a panic
groan	sound made in pain
stutter	say extra letters when speaking
dig	push into
flesh	skin
defied	disobeyed
facilitation	help make something happen
polarization	having very different opinions
cohesiveness	the quality of being together
dissent	disagreement
invulnerable	cannot fail
hatched	created
indispensable	cannot do without
rounding up	gathering
deloused	treated for fleas
pool	a group to draw the participants from
sadistic	liking to cause pain
autonomous	independent, free to choose
inconsistency	always changing, not matched

term	definition
hatred	hate, extreme dislike
accusations	charges for wrong doing
berate	blame
vile	vulgar, filthy
insidious	in a dishonest manner
feminists	people who fight for the rights of women

Thinking Critically

Evaluation

Many Canadians and Americans were surprised when the majority of the people in the Soviet Union rejoiced at the downfall of the communist system. Using what you have learned about attribution bias and conformity, try to explain why many Canadians mistakenly believed that the Soviet population preferred the communist system.

Point/Counterpoint

Prepare a convincing argument supporting each of the following positions:

a. Aggression results largely from biological factors (nature).
b. Aggression is primarily learned (nurture).

Psychology in Your Life

Review the factors influencing impression formation and attraction as discussed in this chapter. Prepare a dual list of behaviours indicating what you should and should not do if you wish to make a better impression on other people and increase their liking for you.

11

PERSONALITY THEORY AND ASSESSMENT

CHAPTER OUTLINE

This outline provides a way to organize your notes from both the text and the lecture. It will also serve as a review for the exam.

Module 11A Sigmund Freud and Psychoanalysis	1. The Conscious, the Preconscious, and the Unconscious: Levels of Awareness 2. The Id, the Ego, and Superego: Warring Components of the Personality

Freud's Conception of the Personality

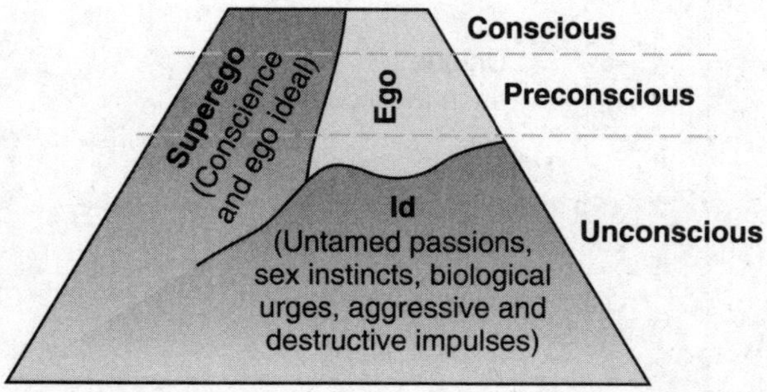

3. Defence Mechanisms: Protecting the Ego

4. The Psychosexual Stages of Development: Centred on the Erogenous Zones

   a. The Oral Stage (Birth to 12 or 18 Months)

   b. The Anal Stage (12 or 18 Months to Age 3)

   c. The Phallic Stage (Ages Three to Five or Six)

   d. The Latency Period (Age Five or Six to Puberty)

   e. The Genital Stage (from Puberty On)

5. Freud's Explanation of Personality

6. Evaluating Freud's Contribution

Module 11B The Neo-Freudians

1. Carl Gustav Jung: Delving into the Collective Unconscious

Jung's Conception of Personality
Like Freud, Carl Jung saw three components in personality. The ego and the personal unconscious are unique to each individual. The collective unconscious is shared by all people and accounts for the similarity of myths and beliefs in diverse cultures.

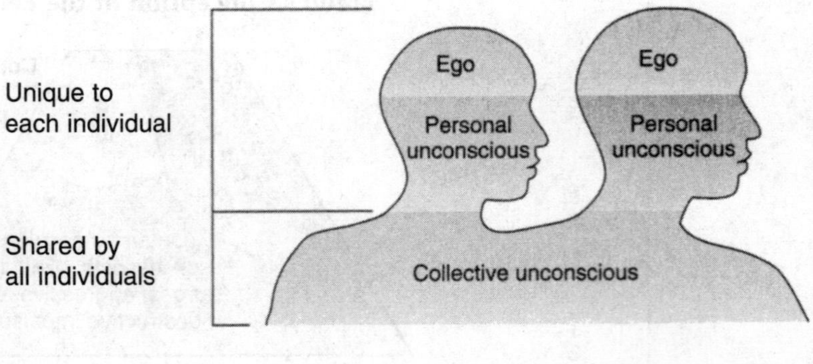

	2. Alfred Adler: Overcoming Inferiority 3. Karen Horney: Champion of Feminine Psychology
Module 11C Trait Theories	1. Gordon Allport: Personality Traits in the Brain 2. Raymond Cattell's 16 Personality Factors 3. Hans Eysenck: Stressing Two Factors 4. The Five-Factor Theory of Personality: The Big Five 5. Evaluating the Trait Perspective
Module 11D Learning Theories and Personality	1. The Behaviourist View of B. F. Skinner 2. The Social-Cognitive Theorists: Expanding the Behaviourist View

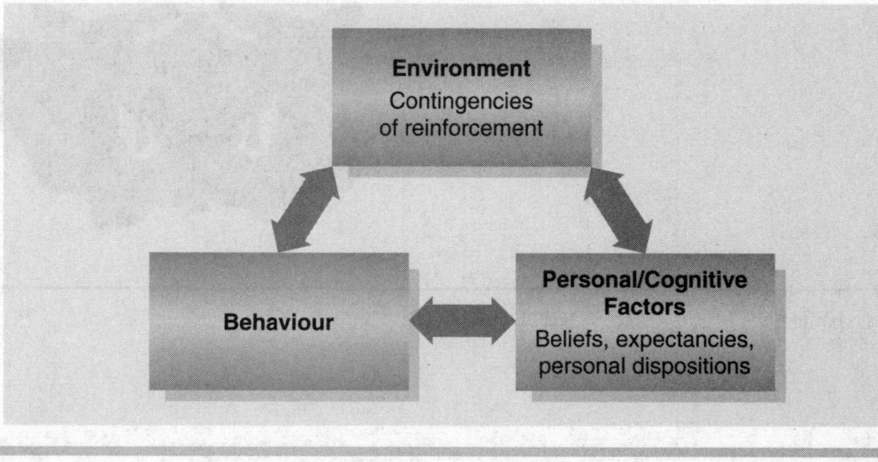

Module 11E Humanistic Personality Theories	1. Abraham Maslow: The Self-Actualizing Person 2. Carl Rogers: The Fully Functioning Person 3. Evaluating the Humanistic Perspective
Module 11F Personality: Is It in the Genes?	1. The Twin Study Method: Studying Identical and Fraternal Twins
Module 11G Personality Assessment	1. Observation, Interviews, and Rating Scales 2. Personality Inventories: Taking Stock 3. Projective Tests: Projections from the Unconscious **An Inkblot similar to One on the Rorschach Inkblot Test** 
Apply It!	Put Your Best Foot Forward

Chapter Learning Objective Questions

Answer the following questions in the space provided and check your answers on the page numbers listed.

11.1 Describe the three levels of awareness in Freud's theory of consciousness. p. 308	
11.2 Explain the roles of the id, ego and superego. p. 308–309	
11.3 Describe the role of defence mechanisms. p. 309	
11.4 Explain fixation and how it can develop during the early stages of psychosexual development. p. 310–312	
11.5 Describe how fixations and the relative balance of the id, ego, and superego influence personality. p. 312	
11.6 Describe the three components of personality according to Jung. p. 314–315	
11.7 Explain archetypes in relation to the collective unconscious. p. 315	
11.8 Compare and contrast Adler's theory of personality with Freud's. p. 355–356	
11.9 Describe an inferiority complex. p. 315	
11.10 Identify factors that Horney believed help us to be psychologically healthy. p. 316	

11.11 Describe traits and trait theories of personality. p. 316	
11.12 Identify the three types of individual traits according to Allport. p. 317	
11.13 Describe surface and source traits, according to Cattell p. 317	
11.14 Identify the three most important dimensions of personality according to Eysenck. p. 318	
11.15 Identify the five factors of the five-factor theory of personality. p. 318–319	
11.16 Explain the origins of abnormal behaviour from Skinner's behaviourist perspective. p. 320	
11.17 Compare and contrast the behaviourist and social-cognitive perspectives. p. 320	
11.18 Identify the components of reciprocal determination and how they interact. p. 320	
11.19 Describe self-efficacy. p. 320–321	
11.20 Describe and contrast internal locus of control and external locus of control. p. 321	

11.21 Describe humanistic psychology. p. 322

11.22 Identify the characteristics that self-actualizing people share. p. 322

11.23 Explain the emergence of the self-concept according to Rogers. p. 322–323

11.24 Describe conditions of worth and its role in our experience of stress and anxiety. p. 323

11.25 Describe behavioural genetics. p. 324

11.26 Describe the findings of twin studies related to the heritability of personality traits. p. 324

11.27 Describe and contrast the influence of the shared environment and the non-shared environment on personality traits. p. 324

11.28 Identify the three major methods used in personality assessment. p. 324

11.29 Describe the use of observation, interviews, and rating scales in personality assessment. p. 325

11.30 Describe the MMPI-2, the JPI, and the use of inventories to assess personality. p. 325

11.31 Explain how projective tests are used to gain insight into personality. p. 326

Practice Multiple-Choice Test

After studying the text and completing the Study Guide activities, answer these questions to determine if you need to review any areas before your exam.

1. The definition of personality is based on observations that people:
   a. possess stable traits that uniquely distinguish them from others.
   b. are uniquely defined by traits that do not stabilize over time.
   c. differ only superficially from each other, and are basically alike.
   d. have stable traits that make them psychologically indistinguishable.

2. Sigmund Freud's theory is called:
   a. dynamic psychology.
   b. analytical psychology.
   c. psychoanalysis.
   d. psychic determinism.

3. According to Carl Rogers the main source for human emotional problems comes from people
   a. giving us a negative ego.
   b. setting up conditions of worth focus.
   c. being accepting and open with us too often.
   d. ignoring our behaviour.

4. The psychoanalytic system of the personality, which contains the life and death instincts and operates on the pleasure principle, is called the:
   a. ego
   b. id
   c. superego
   d. preconscious

5. The primary function of the ego is to:
   a. satisfy the desires of the id in a socially acceptable way.
   b. deny and overpower the id
   c. shift energy from the id to the superego
   d. promote behaviour that is unselfish and ethical

6. The superego is described as:
   a. an internalization of the moral teaching of our parents and society.
   b. a reality-oriented censor of behaviour.
   c. a manifestation of the instinct for survival of the species.
   d. a product of human evolution.

7. In the psychoanalytic view, what technique is used by the ego to protect against anxiety and to maintain self-esteem?
   a. free association
   b. fixation
   c. defence mechanism
   d. death instinct

8. Freud would say that the memories that have been removed from consciousness because they were too anxiety-provoking have been:
   a. repressed.
   b. expunged.
   c. repulsed.
   d. excised.

9. Ira denies his hatred for his brother Justin and claims that it is Justin who hates him. Ira may be using the defence mechanism called:
   a. rationalization.
   b. projection.
   c. sublimation.
   d. reaction formation.

10. Tony has just been informed that he is HIV positive. He refuses to believe it and insists that his test must have been confused with another's. Tony is probably using:
    a. reaction formation.
    b. sublimation.
    c. regression.
    d. denial.

11. Regression is defined as:
   a. attributing our own undesirable thoughts or behaviour to others.
   b. making excuses to justify our failures or mistakes.
   c. taking out our frustrations on a less threatening person or object.
   d. reverting to a behaviour that might have reduced anxiety at an earlier stage of development.

12. Freud theorized that the psychosexual stages occur in the order of:
   a. anal; oral; genital; phallic.
   b. oral; anal; phallic; genital.
   c. genital; anal; oral; phallic.
   d. anal; phallic; oral; genital.

13. According to Freud, the most important years in personality development were:
   a. from birth to 5 or 6.
   b. from 5 or 6 to puberty.
   c. adolescence.
   d. adulthood.

14. In Jung's theory, the inherited part of the personality, which stores the universal experiences of mankind is the:
   a. personal unconscious.
   b. impersonal unconscious.
   c. collective unconscious.
   d. universal unconscious.

15. People who see themselves as being able to perform competently and successfully in whatever they attempt, have what Bandura calls
   a. high self-regard
   b. a positive ego-picture
   c. reinforced behaviour
   d. high self-efficacy

16. ______________ believed that we are driven by a need to overcome and compensate for inferiority feelings and strive for superiority and significance.
   a. Sigmund Freud
   b. Carl Jung
   c. Alfred Adler
   d. Karen Horney

17. Karen Horney argued that women really want the same opportunities and the rights and privileges afforded males in society. This view was meant to replace Freud's concept of:
   a. defence mechanisms.
   b. anxiety.
   c. superego.
   d. penis envy.

18. The particular ways we respond to the environment that remain fairly constant over time are called ____________.
   a. norms
   b. egos
   c. traits
   d. clusters

19. According to Allport's theory, which of the following refers to a trait that is so strong a part of a person's life that he or she becomes identified with the trait?
   a. cardinal trait
   b. central trait
   c. primary trait
   d. ordinal trait

20. You tell your friend that you enjoy his company because he is fun-loving, intelligent, generous, and kind. According to Cattell, what type of traits are those?
   a. surface traits
   b. source traits
   c. primary traits
   d. secondary traits

21. Hans Eysenck's trait dimension of emotional stability versus instability is also known as:
   a. extroversion.
   b. introversion.
   c. psychoticism.
   d. neuroticism.

22. According to B. F. Skinner, which of the following ideas about personality was acceptable?
   a Personality is a useful concept.
   b. We initiate and direct our own behaviour.
   c. Rewards and punishments shape our behaviour.
   d. Abnormal behaviour is primarily biological in origin.

23. Sigmund Freud proposed that the psyche or the personality is comprised of three systems:
    a. conscious, unconscious, preconscious
    b. id, ego, superego
    c. id, ego, alterego
    d. pleasure, reality, conscience

24. _______________ is arrested development at a psychosexual stage occurring because of excessive gratification or frustration at that stage.
    a. Fixation
    b. Sublimation
    c. Displacement
    d. Reaction formation

25. Alfred Adler (1870–1937) _______________ with most of Freud's basic beliefs; on many points his views were_________.
    a. agreed; the same
    b. disagreed; the exact opposite
    c. disagreed; however, the same
    d. agreed; different

Answers to Multiple-Choice Questions

Question Number	Answer	Explanation for application questions
1.	a.	
2.	c.	
3.	b.	
4.	b.	
5.	a.	The ego attempts to find balance between the demands of the id and the strict rules of the superego.
6.	a.	
7.	c.	
8.	a.	
9.	b.	Projection is attributing one's own undesirable thoughts, impulses, traits, or behaviours to others.
10.	d.	
11.	d.	
12.	b.	
13.	a.	
14.	c.	
15.	d.	
16.	c.	
17.	d.	Karen Horney believed women do not envy men's penises, as Freud thought, but rather envy the privileges men enjoy.
18.	c.	
19.	a.	
20.	a.	
21.	d.	
22.	c.	
23.	b.	
24.	a.	
25.	b.	

Glossary for Text Language Enhancement

Students identified the following words from the text as needing more explanation. This page can be cut out, folded in half, and used as a bookmark for this chapter.

term	definition
exempted	does not apply to them
equivalent	equal to
controversial	unsettled, debatable
heinous	terrible
impulse	stimulus, drive
minimize	make very small
exaggerate	make larger than it really is
inherited	inborn, born with
gratify	satisfy
tyrannical	mean, nasty
irrational	not reasonable
compatible	capable of getting along well together
lurk	hide
traumatic	terrible, very bad
rechannel	put in another area
puberty	body changes to adult
fixation	stuck in a spot
overindulgence	too much
gullibility	too trusting
sarcasm	hurtful words
stingy	selfish
stubborn	not willing to change
rigid	very firm
culminate	to end in
replicated	done again
gratify	satisfy
envy	jealousy
myths	stories, legends
tendency	way
consistent	always the same
essence	the basic, perhaps the most important, part of something
introspective	tending to look into one's own mind, emotions, or reactions
instability	unsteady, not stable
negligent	fail to do the right thing
vindictive	revengeful in spirit
boisterous	loud
easygoing	not easily angered

term	definition
reciprocal severest	given or felt in return most harsh

Thinking Critically

Evaluation

In your opinion, which personality theory is the most accurate, reasonable, and realistic? Which is the least accurate, reasonable, and realistic? Support your answers.

Point/Counterpoint

Are personality characteristics mostly learned? Or are they mostly transmitted through the genes? Using what you have learned in this chapter and other evidence you can gather, make a case for each position. Support your answers with research and expert opinion.

Psychology in Your Life

Consider your own behaviour and personality attributes from the standpoint of each of the theories: psychoanalysis, trait theory, and the learning, humanistic, and genetic perspectives. Which theory or theories best explain your personality? Why?

12

HEALTH AND STRESS

CHAPTER OUTLINE

This outline provides a way to organize your notes from both the text and the lecture. It will also serve as a review for the exam.

Module 12A Theories of Stress	1. Hans Selye and the General Adaptation Syndrome

The Biopsychosocial Model of Health and Wellness

The biopsychosocial model focuses on health as well as illness and holds that both are determined by a combination of biological, psychological, and social factors. Most health psychologists endorse the biopsychosocial model.

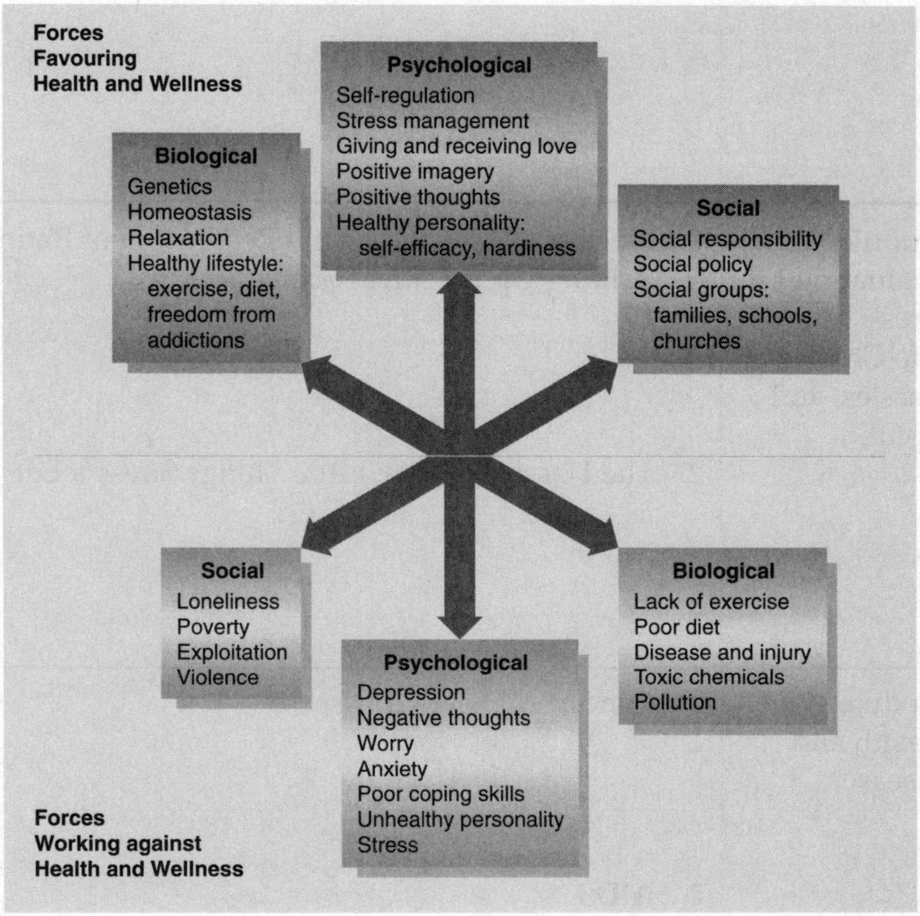

2. Richard Lazarus's Cognitive Theory of Stress

Module 12B Sources of Stress: The Common and the Extreme

1. Everyday Sources of Stress

- Unpredictability and Lack of Control: Factors That Increase Stress
- Racism and Stress

2. Catastrophic Events and Chronic Intense Stress

3. Post-Traumatic Stress Disorder

Module 12C Coping with Stress	1. Problem-Focused and Emotion-Focused Coping
Module 12D Evaluating Life Stress: Major Life Changes, Hassles, and Uplifts	1. Holmes and Rahe's Social Readjustment Rating Scale: Adding Up the Stress Scores 2. The Hassles of Life: Little Things Stress a Lot
Module 12E Health and Disease	1. Cancer: A Dreaded Disease 2. AIDS 3. Stress and the Immune System 4. Personal Factors Reducing the Impact of Stress and Illness

Module 12F Your Lifestyle and Your Health	1. Smoking: Hazardous to Your Health 2. Alcohol: A Problem for Millions 3. Exercise: Keeping Fit Is Healthy
Apply It!	Interpreting Health Information on the Internet: 1. There are no rules governing what is published on the internet. 2. Consider the source. 3. Get a second opinion. 4. Examine references. 5. How current is the information? 6. Is it too good to be true?

Chapter Learning Objective Questions

Answer the following questions in the space provided and check your answers on the page numbers listed.

12.1 Describe Selye's concept of general adaptation syndrome. p. 337	
12.2 Describe the physiological responses during the alarm, resistance, and exhaustion stages of general adaptation. p. 337–334	
12.3 Explain the four phases of response to a potentially stressful event according to Lazarus's cognitive theory of stress and coping. p. 238	
12.4 Describe the primary and secondary appraisal processes that occur in response to a potentially stressful event. p. 338–339	
12.5 Describe approach-approach, approach-avoidance, and avoidance-avoidance conflicts in motivation. p. 340	
12.6 Explain how the unpredictability of, and lack of control over, a stressor affects its impact. p. 340	
12.7 Explain the relationship between racism and the experience of stress. p. 340	
12.8 Identify the stages in which victims tend to react to catastrophic events. p. 341	
12.9 Describe the symptoms that characterize post-traumatic stress disorder. p. 341–342	
12.10 Describe coping. p. 342	

12.11 Explain and compare problem-focused and emotion-focused coping. p. 342–343	
12.12 Describe an effective stress management strategy. p. 343	
12.13 Describe what the Social Readjustment Rating Scale is designed to measure. p. 343	
12.14 Explain the connection between life stress and health problems. p. 344	
12.15 Explain the balance between daily hassles and uplifts in the experience of stress. p. 344–345	
12.16 Identify positive strategies for coping with cancer and cancer treatment. p. 346–347	
12.17 Describe the psychological impact of HIV infection and AIDS and strategies for coping psychologically. p. 347–348	
12.18 Describe psychoneuroimmunology and the effects of stress and depression on the immune system. p. 347–348	
12.19 Explain the role of optimism in physical health. p. 348	
12.20 Discuss social support as a factor that contributes to better health. p. 348	

12.21 Explain factors that constitute an unhealthy lifestyle. p. 349

12.22 Identify factors apart from the physical addiction that can diminish a smoker's ability to quit smoking. p. 349–350

12.23 Describe the disease model of alcoholism and the limitations of this model. p. 350

12.24 Identify the benefits of regular exercise to promoting better health. p. 350–351

Chart Completion Exercise

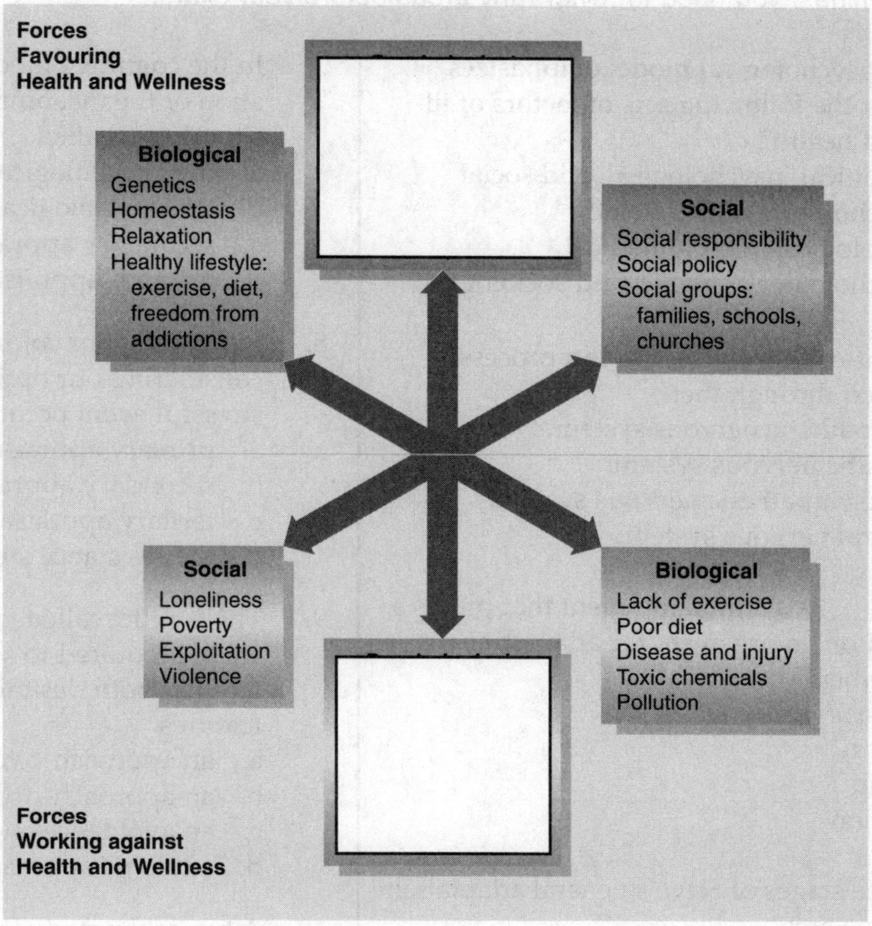

Practice Multiple-Choice Test

After studying the text and completing the Study Guide activities, answer these questions to determine if you need to review any areas before your exam.

1. The biopsychological model emphasizes which of the following sets of factors of illness and health?
   a. biological, psychological, and social
   b. psychological and genetic
   c. sociological and biomedical
   d. psychological, genetic, and sociological

2. The fight-or-flight response is a process controlled through the:
   a. sympathetic nervous system.
   b. somatic nervous system.
   c. parasympathetic nervous system.
   d. central nervous system.

3. A ________ is a stimuli or event that places a demand on an organism for adaptation or readjustment.
   a. stressor
   b. stress
   c. strain
   d. tension

4. The three stages of Selye's general adaptation syndrome are:
   a. perception, response, and recovery.
   b. perception, interpretation, and flight.
   c. alarm, resistance, and exhaustion.
   d. adaptation, modification, and adoption.

5. During what stage of the general adaptation syndrome is susceptibility to illness increased?
   a. alarm
   b. terminal
   c. resistance
   d. exhaustion

6. Some psychologists believe that Selye failed to consider the:
   a. physiological component of stress.
   b. psychological component of stress.
   c. health consequences of stress.
   d. impact of stress on animals.

7. In the cognitive model of stress, the evaluation of the meaning and significance of a situation is called:
   a. the psychological stressor.
   b. the physiological stressor.
   c. secondary appraisal.
   d. primary appraisal.

8. Evaluating our coping resources and considering our options in dealing with a stressful event occurs during:
   a. primary appraisal.
   b. secondary appraisal.
   c. tertiary appraisal.
   d. the resistance stage.

9. The conflict called _____ occurs whenever we are required to select an alternative that has both desirable and undesirable features.
   a. an approach–avoidance conflict
   b. an approach–approach conflict
   c. an avoidance–avoidance conflict
   d. a double approach–avoidance conflict

10. A typical immediate reaction to a catastrophic event is for a person to be:
    a. in a state of panic.
    b. highly emotional.
    c. dazed, stunned, and emotionally numb.
    d. composed enough to help others.

11. People suffering from posttraumatic stress disorder may experience all of the following EXCEPT:
    a. They startle easily.
    b. They are anxious.
    c. They have nightmares and flashbacks.
    d. Their symptoms are not readily apparent.

12. Problem-focused coping strategies are most useful in situations that are:
    a. moderately stressful.
    b. extremely stressful.
    c. unchangeable.
    d. changeable.

13. An example of emotion-focused coping is ________________.
    a. studying or working harder
    b. humour
    c. talking the problem over with an expert
    d. writing a letter to your MP

14. Well-functioning people use:
    a. mostly problem-focused coping.
    b. mostly emotion-focused coping.
    c. a combination of problem-focused and emotion-focused coping.
    d. a minimum of problem-focused and emotion-focused coping.

15. When you are experiencing a lot of stress you can reduce the impact of the stress by helping others. How does this work?
    a. those you help will take your stress away
    b. it makes you feel less like a victim and more like a contributor
    c. you cannot think of two things at once, helping and your distress
    d. it will not help, your stress is unchangeable

16. According to Holmes and Rahe, persons who experience a number of major life changes over the course of a year are likely to have what kind of experience in the next two years?
    a. change jobs more frequently than usual
    b. have a high probability of getting a divorce
    c. have a high probability of committing a crime
    d. experience more health problems than usual

17. According to Lazarus, what usually causes the average person the most stress?
    a. major life changes
    b. catastrophic events
    c. hassles
    d. approach-avoidance conflicts

18. The term ____________ refers to the positive experiences in life that can neutralize the effects of many of the hassles.
    a. highs
    b. uplifts
    c. peak experiences
    d. destressors

19. The research on coping with the distress of cancer has found that ____________ reduces the distress.
    a. a pessimistic outlook
    b. surrendering to the disuse
    c. social support
    d. a serious attitude

20. What is the relationship between stress and the immune system?
    a. stress helps the immune system become tough
    b. lower stress levels weaken the immune system
    c. the immune system prevents stress responses
    d. high levels of stress are related to lower immune activity

21. According to Parrott (1993) why do most people smoke?
    a. it serves as a coping mechanism for regulating moods
    b. they enjoy the activity
    c. they are simple copying other people's behaviour
    d. for status and image enhancement

22. Research on environmental influences leading to alcohol abuse or alcoholism suggests:
    a. genetics play the major role in causing the problem.
    b. all alcoholics can learn to drink socially.
    c. sons of alcoholics are less likely to drink if they are adopted into another family than sons of non-alcoholics.
    d. behavioural, social, and cultural factors play a role in alcoholism.

23. When we assess an event as stressful, we engage in a ________________ appraisal. During this process, if we judge the situation to be within our control, we make an evaluation of our available coping resources and then decide how to deal with the stressful event.
a. resistance
b. primary
c. secondary
d. tertiary

24. ________________ contends that it is not the stressor itself that causes stress, but a person's perception of the stressor.
a. Richard Lazarus
b. Hans Selye
c. B. F. Skinner
d. Brenda Milner

25. Holmes and Rahe maintain that there is a connection between the degree of ___________ and major health problems.
a. marital stress
b. work stress
c. social adjustment to life changes
d. emotion-focused coping

Answers to Multiple-Choice Questions

Question Number	Answer	Explanation for application questions
1.	a.	
2.	a.	
3.	a.	
4.	c.	
5.	d.	
6.	b.	
7.	d.	
8.	b.	
9.	a.	
10.	c.	
11.	d.	
12.	d.	
13.	b.	
14.	c.	
15.	b.	
16.	d.	
17.	c.	
18.	b.	
19.	c.	
20.	d.	
21.	a.	
22.	d.	
23.	b.	
24.	a.	
25.	c.	

Glossary for Text Language Enhancement

Students identified the following words from the text as needing more explanation. This page can be cut out, folded in half, and used as a bookmark for this chapter.

term	definition
debilitating	weakening
degenerative disease	an illness that causes a continued decline in health
on the verge	just about to do something
brooding	dwelling on
exhilaration	excitement
depleted	exhausted
appraisal	analysis
orthodox	agreeing with the established beliefs
catastrophic	horrible
aimlessly	without purpose
disintegration	separate into parts
cope	deal with
myriad	a large number of things
scourge	inflicts severe suffering
succumb	open to
craving	strong desire (want)
total abstinence	not using any alcohol at all
strenuous	difficult

Thinking Critically

Evaluation

Can people always cure themselves of illnesses? What are the limits to what people can do to help themselves?

Point/Counterpoint

Prepare two arguments, one supporting the position that alcoholism is a genetically inherited disease, and the other supporting the position that alcoholism is not a medical disease but results from learning.

Psychology in Your Life

Choose several stress-producing incidents from your own life and explain what problem-focused and emotion-focused coping strategies you used. From the knowledge you have gained in this chapter, list other coping strategies that might have been more effective.

13

PSYCHOLOGICAL DISORDERS

CHAPTER OUTLINE

This outline provides a way to organize your notes from both the text and the lecture. It will also serve as a review for the exam.

Module 13A What Is Abnormal?	1. Perspectives on the Causes and Treatment of Psychological Disorders a. Biological Perspective b. Psychodynamic Perspective c. Learning Perspective d. Cognitive Perspective e. Humanistic Perspective

	2. Defining and Classifying Psychological Disorders
Module 13B Anxiety Disorders: When Anxiety Is Extreme	1. Generalized Anxiety Disorder 2. Panic Disorder 3. Phobias: Persistent, Irrational Fears 4. Obsessive Compulsive Disorder
Module 13C Somatoform and Dissociative Disorders	1. Somatoform Disorders: Physical Symptoms with Psychological Causes a. Hypochondriasis b. Conversion Disorder: When Thoughts and Fears Can Paralyze 2. Dissociative Disorders: Mental Escapes a. Dissociative Amnesia: "Who Am I?" b. Dissociative Fugue: "Where Did I Go and What Did I Do?"

c. Dissociative Identity Disorder: Multiple Personality

Module 13D Schizophrenia	1. The Symptoms of Schizophrenia: Many and Varied a. Positive Symptoms • Hallucinations • Delusions • Disturbances in the Form of Thought or Speech • Grossly Disorganized Behaviour • Inappropriate Affect b. Negative Symptoms • Social withdrawal, apathy, loss of motivation, lack of goal-directed activity, limited speech, slow movements, poor hygiene and grooming, poor problem-solving abilities, and a distorted sense of time c. Brain Abnormalities in Some Schizophrenics 2. Types of Schizophrenia a. Catatonic b. Disorganized c. Paranoid d. Undifferentiated

3. The Causes of Schizophrenia

a. Genetic Inheritance

Genetic Similarity and Probability of Developing Schizophrenia

Research strongly indicates a genetic factor operating in many cases of schizophrenia. Identical twins have identical genes, and if one twin develops schizophrenia, the other twin has a 46 percent chance of developing it also. In fraternal twins the chance is only 14 percent. A person with one schizophrenic parent has a 13 percent chance of developing schizophrenia, but a 46 percent chance if both parents are schizophrenic. (Data from Nicol and Gottesman 1983.)

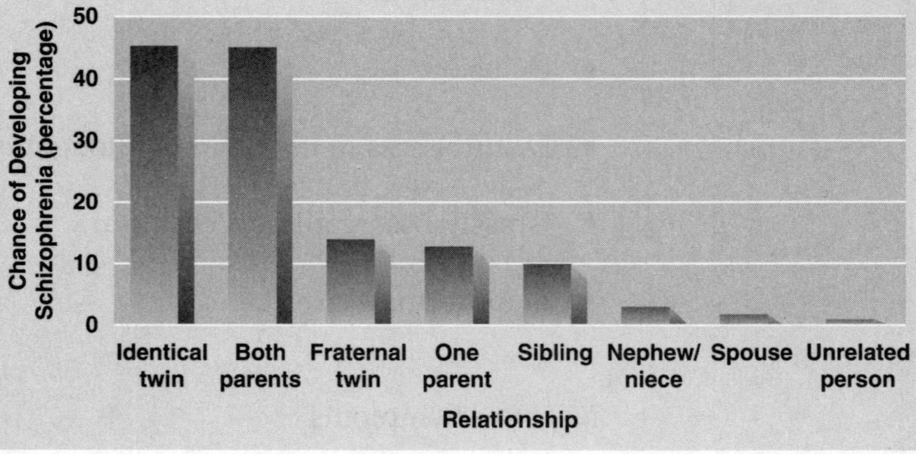

b. Excessive Dopamine Activity

4. Gender and Schizophrenia

Module 13E Mood Disorders

1. Depressive Disorders and Bipolar Disorder: Emotional Highs, and Lows

a. Major Depressive Disorder

b. Seasonal Depression

c. Bipolar Disorder

	2. Causes of Major Depressive Disorder and Bipolar Disorder a. The Biological Perspective b. The Cognitive Perspective
Module 13F Other Psychological Disorders	1. Personality Disorders: Troublesome Behaviour Patterns • Antisocial Personality Disorder 2. Sexual and Gender Identity Disorders
Apply It!	Overcoming the Fear of Public Speaking

Chapter Learning Objective Questions

Answer the following questions in the space provided and check your answers on the page numbers listed.

13.1 Identify criteria for differentiating normal from abnormal behaviour. p. 358	
13.2 Identify five current perspectives that attempt to explain the causes of psychological disorders. p. 359	
13.3 Describe what the DSM-IV-TR is used for and how it assists mental health professionals. p. 359	
13.4 Describe and contrast neurosis and psychosis. p. 359–361	
13.5 Describe and contrast normal and abnormal anxiety. p. 362	
13.6 Describe generalized anxiety disorder. p. 362	
13.7 Identify the social and health consequences of panic disorder. p. 363	
13.8 Identify and describe the characteristics of three categories of phobias. p. 363–364	
13.9 Describe the obsessions and compulsions that characterize obsessive-compulsive disorder. p. 364–365	
13.10 Describe and contrast hypochondriasis and conversion disorder. p. 366	

13.11 Describe dissociative disorders. p. 366	
13.12 Compare and contrast dissociative amnesia and dissociative fugue. p. 367	
13.13 Identify the symptoms and causes of dissociative identity disorder. p. 367	
13.14 Describe the major positive symptoms of schizophrenia and contrast these with the negative symptoms. p. 368–369	
13.15 Identify brain abnormalities that have been associated with schizophrenia. p. 369	
13.16 Identify the four subtypes of schizophrenia. p. 370	
13.17 Explain the cause of schizophrenia according to the diathesis-stress model. p. 371	
13.18 Identify the symptoms that characterize major depressive disorder. p. 372	
13.19 Contrast major depressive disorder and dysthymia. p. 372–373	
13.20 Describe a major manic episode and its negative effects. p. 373–374	
13.21 Explain the role of genetic inheritance and neurotransmitters in major depressive disorder. p. 374	

13.22 Describe the distortions in thinking that characterize depression. p. 374	
13.23 Describe personality disorders. p. 375	
13.24 Describe and compare Cluster A, Cluster B, and Cluster C personality disorders. p. 375–376	
13.25 Identify the symptoms associated with borderline personality disorder. p. 375	
13.26 Describe two categories of sexual disorders. p. 377	

Practice Multiple-Choice Test

After studying the text and completing the Study Guide activities, answer these questions to determine if you need to review any areas before your exam.

1. All of the following are true about the distinction between normal and abnormal behaviour EXCEPT:
   a. A person might be considered normal in one culture and abnormal in another.
   b. Not all people whose behaviour is abnormal experience personal distress.
   c. The most widely used criterion for committing people to an institution is whether they are a danger to themselves or others.
   d. It is relatively easy to differentiate normal behaviour from abnormal behaviour.

2. A psychologist is convinced that abnormal behaviours arise from structural abnormalities and chemical imbalances in the brain. His view of abnormal behaviour is most consistent with the:
   a. psychodynamic perspective.
   b. humanistic perspective.
   c. cognitive perspective.
   d. biological perspective.

3. Which perspective suggests that unconscious sexual or aggressive conflicts in early childhood experiences are the cause of abnormal behaviour?
   a. cognitive perspective
   b. humanistic perspective
   c. psychodynamic perspective
   d. biological perspective

4. Which is a suggested cause of abnormal behaviour from the cognitive perspective?
   a. faulty learning
   b. early childhood experiences
   c. unconscious, unresolved conflicts
   d. faulty thinking

5. Which of the following perspectives suggests that psychological disorders arise from the blocking of a person's natural tendency toward self-actualization?
   a. the humanistic perspective
   b. the learning perspective
   c. the biological perspective
   d. the cognitive perspective

6. The DSM-IV-TR is a manual published by the American Psychiatric Association that is used to:
   a. diagnose mental disorders.
   b. explain the causes of mental disorders.
   c. outline treatments for various mental disorders.
   d. assess the effectiveness of treatment programs.

7. The diagnosis of generalized anxiety disorder applies to people who:
   a. are feeling bad about their anxiety.
   b. are experiencing an unusual change in their lives that is causing anxiety.
   c. are having irrational thoughts and suicidal tendencies.
   d. are experiencing excessive anxiety that they cannot control.

8. The disorder characterized by recurrent and unpredictable attacks of anxiety, panic, or terror is known as:
   a. panic disorder.
   b. obsessive-compulsive disorder.
   c. generalized anxiety disorder.
   d. phobia.

9. A persistent, irrational fear of some object, situation, or activity that a person feels compelled to avoid is called:
   a. an avoidance response.
   b. a phobia.
   c. a panic attack.
   d. an obsession.

10. A persistent recurring involuntary thought, image, or impulse that invades consciousness and causes great distress is called:
    a. a hallucination.
    c. a delusion.
    b. an obsession.
    d. a compulsion.

11. A behaviour that a person feels driven to perform is called:
   a. a hallucination.
   b. an obsession.
   c. a delusion.
   d. a compulsion.

12. People who are preoccupied with their health and convinced they have some serious disorder despite reassurances from medical doctors to the contrary are usually suffering from:
   a. conversion disorder.
   b. psychogenic illness.
   c. psychosomatic neurosis.
   d. hypochondriasis.

13. Becky saw her brother get killed at a restaurant. She has not been able to see since that night even though doctors say there is nothing wrong with her eyes. Becky is probably suffering from:
   a. conversion disorder.
   b. an anxiety disorder.
   c. a phobia.
   d. a dissociative disorder.

14. What is the disorder in which two or more distinct personalities exist in a person, each personality taking over at different times?
   a. dissociative amnesia
   b. split personality
   c. dissociative identity disorder
   d. schizophrenia

15. A(n) _________ is occurring when a person sees, hears, smells, or tastes something when there is nothing causing the sensation.
   a. a hallucination
   b. a delusion
   c. an obsession
   d. a compulsion

16. Delusions are ___________ while hallucinations are ___________.
   a. irrational thoughts; unusual sensations
   b. unusual sensations; irrational thoughts
   c. false beliefs; imaginary sensations
   d. imaginary sensations; false beliefs

17. Someone with a diagnosis of ___________ believes people are after him and trying to hurt him, even though this is not true.
   a. catatonic schizophrenia
   b. disorganized schizophrenia
   c. undifferentiated schizophrenia
   d. paranoid schizophrenia

18. Drugs effective in treating schizophrenia:
   a. block the action of norepinephrine in the brain.
   b. reduce blood flow in the brain.
   c. block the action of dopamine in the brain.
   d. increase melatonin levels in the brain.

19. The most frequently occurring major psychological disorder is:
   a. phobias.
   b. schizophrenia.
   c. bipolar disorder.
   d. depression.

20. What is the term for a period of extreme elation, euphoria, and hyperactivity, which is often accompanied by delusions of grandeur?
   a. seasonal euphoric episode
   b. delusional euphoric episode
   c. manic episode
   d. hyperinflationary state

21. Low levels of neurotransmitters such as norepinephrine and serotonin are associated with ___________; high levels of these same neurotransmitters are associated with ___________.
   a. mania; schizophrenia
   b. depression; schizophrenia
   c. depression; mania
   d. mania; depression

22. A disorder in which a bizarre practice is necessary for sexual gratification is called a(n):
   a. sexual dysfunction.
   b. impaired sexual performance.
   c. paranormia.
   d. inorgasmia.

23. Panic disorder is characterized by recurrent, unpredictable panic attacks that cause apprehension about ___________.
    a. the future
    b. the occurrence and consequences of further attacks
    c. specific phobias
    d. physical exams

24. A somatoform disorder in which a loss of motor or sensory functioning in some part of the body has no physical cause but solves some psychological problem is called __________ disorder.
    a. hypochondiasis
    b. conversion
    c. dissociative
    d. amnesic

25. Positive symptoms of schizophrenia include:
    a. hallucinations
    b. social withdrawal
    c. apathy
    d. loss of motivation

Answers to Multiple-Choice Questions

Question Number	Answer	Explanation for application questions
1.	d.	
2.	d.	
3.	c.	
4.	d.	
5.	a.	
6.	a.	
7.	d.	
8.	a.	
9.	b.	
10.	b.	
11.	d.	
12.	d.	
13.	a.	
14.	c.	
15.	a.	
16.	c.	
17.	d.	
18.	c.	
19.	d.	
20.	c.	
21.	c.	
22.	a.	
23.	b.	
24.	b.	
25.	a.	

Glossary for Text Language Enhancement

Students identified the following words from the text as needing more explanation. This page can be cut out, folded in half, and used as a bookmark for this chapter.

term	definition
advocacy	acting on behalf of others, to help
clear-cut	obvious
obsolete	gone out of use
vague	not specific
prompts	helps
unduly	unnecessarily
sheds	gives
clumsy	to fall easily
catch-all	contains many different types
raw	sore
stabbing	putting a knife into
intolerable	too painful to deal with
alter-	other personality
forth	forward
menacing	threatening
dishevelled	unclean; not orderly
agitation	becoming forceful, violent
stupor	a state in which the mind and senses are dulled
grimaces	twisting of the face
incoherent	not making sense
elation	extreme happiness
despair	extreme unhappiness
disproportionately	in a manner that is not equal
recurrence	happening again
euphoria	feeling very good
wound up	full of energy
spending sprees	spending a lot of money
enraged	feeling extreme anger
remorse	being sorry for something
gender	male or female

Thinking Critically

Evaluation

Some psychological disorders are more common in women (depression, agoraphobia, and specific phobia), and some are more common in men (antisocial personality disorder and substance-related disorders). Give some possible reasons why such gender differences exist in these disorders. Support your answer.

Point/Counterpoint

There is continuing controversy over whether specific psychological disorders are chiefly biological in origin (nature) or result primarily from learning and experience (nurture). Select any two disorders from this chapter and prepare arguments for both nature and nurture for both disorders.

Psychology in Your Life

Formulate a specific plan for your own life that will help you recognize and avoid the five cognitive traps that contribute to unhealthy thinking. You might enlist the help of a friend to monitor your negative statements.

14

THERAPIES

CHAPTER OUTLINE

This outline provides a way to organize your notes from both the text and the lecture. It will also serve as a review for the exam.

Module 14A Insight Therapies	1. Psychodynamic Therapies: Freud Revisited a. Psychoanalysis: From the Couch of Freud b. Psychodynamic Therapy Today: The New View c. Criticisms of Psychoanalytic Therapy 2. The Humanistic Therapy a. Person-Centred Therapy: The Patient Becomes the Person b. Gestalt Therapy: Getting in Touch with Your Feelings

Module 14B Relationship Therapies: Therapies Emphasizing Interaction with Others	1. Couples Therapy: Healing Our Relationships 2. Family Therapy 3. Group Therapy: Helping One at a Time, Together 4. Group Help of a Different Sort
Module 14C Behaviour Therapies: Unlearning the Old, Learning the New	1. Behaviour Modification Techniques Based on Operant Conditioning a. Token Economies: What Would You Do for a Token? b. Time Out: All Alone with No Reinforcers c. Stimulus Satiation: Too Much of a Good Thing d. The Effectiveness of Operant Approaches: Do They Work? 2. Therapies Based on Classical Conditioning

a. Systematic Desensitization: Overcoming Fears One Step at a Time

b. Flooding: Confronting Our Fears All at Once

c. Exposure and Response Prevention: Cutting the Tie that Binds Fears and Rituals

d. Aversion Therapy: Making Us Sick to Make Us Better

3. Therapies Based on Observational Learning: Just Watch This!

- Participant Modelling

Module 14D Cognitive Therapies: It's the Thought That Counts

1. Rational-Emotive Therapy: Human Misery—The Legacy of False Beliefs

The ABCs of Albert Ellis's Rational-Emotive Therapy

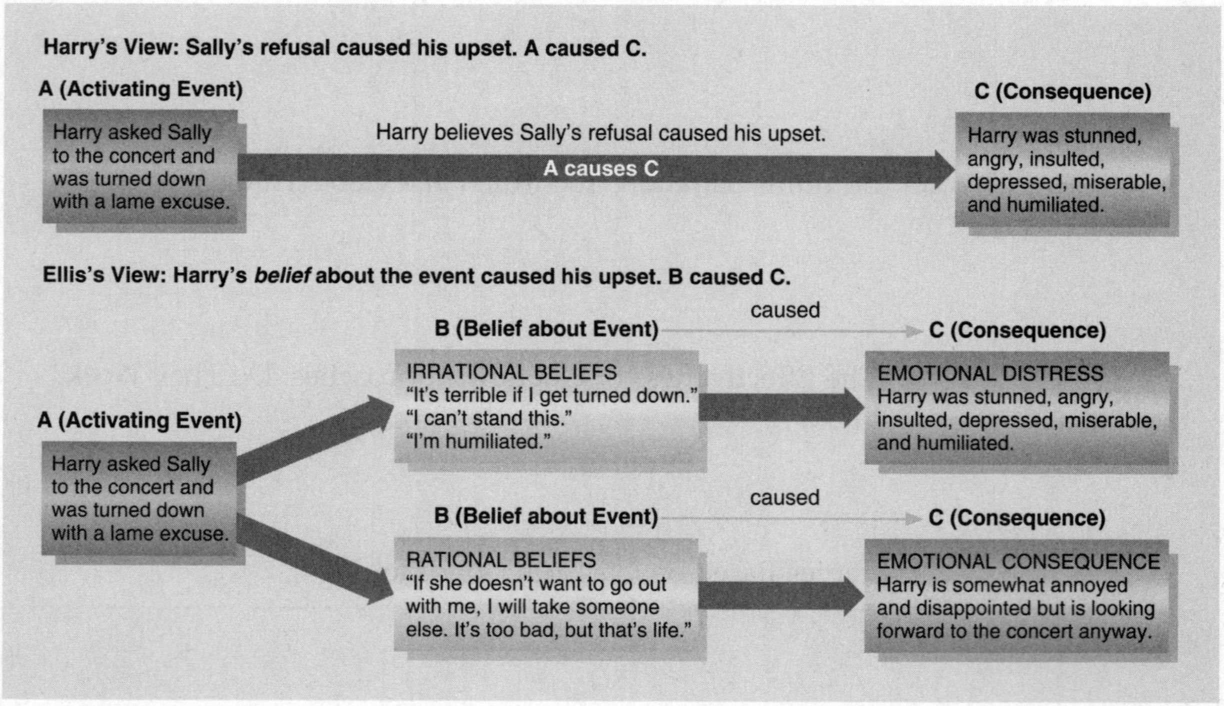

	2. Beck's Cognitive Therapy: Overcoming the "Power of Negative Thinking" 3. Cognitive Behavioural Therapy: Changes in Thought Change Behaviour
Module 14E Eye Movement Desensitization and Reprocessing (EMDR)	
Module 14F The Biological Therapies	1. Drug Therapy: Pills for Psychological Ills a. Antipsychotic Drugs b. Antidepressant Drugs c. Lithium: A Natural Salt that Evens Moods d. The Minor Tranquillizers e. Some Problems with Drug Therapy 2. Electroconvulsive Therapy: The Controversy Continues a. The Side Effects of ECT 3. Psychosurgery: Cutting to Cure
Module 14G Therapies and Therapists: Many Choices	1. Evaluating the Therapies: Do They Work? 2. Mental Health Professionals: How Do They Differ? 3. Therapy and Race, Ethnicity, and Gender
Apply It!	Choosing a Therapist

Chapter Learning Objective Questions

Answer the following questions in the space provided and check your answers on the page numbers listed.

14.1 Define psychotherapy and insight therapy. p. 386	
14.2 Identify the four basic techniques of psychoanalysis and how they are used to help patients. p. 386–387	
14.3 Explain similarities and differences among person-centered and Gestalt therapies. p. 387–388	
14.4 Describe the characteristics that define relationship therapies. p. 388–389	
14.5 Explain the differences between traditional and integrated behavioural couple therapies. p. 389	
14.6 Understand the goals of family therapy. p. 389	
14.7 Identify the advantages of group therapy. p. 390	
14.8 Define behavioural modification. p. 390	
14.9 Identify three operant-based behaviour modification techniques and explain how each changes behaviour. p. 391	
14.10 Identify four therapies based on classical conditioning and explain how they are implemented. p. 392–393	

14.11 Understand how modeling helps people overcome fears. p. 394

14.12 Define cognitive therapies. p. 395

14.13 Explain what is meant by the ABCs of rational-emotive therapy. p. 395

14.14 Describe how Beck's cognitive therapy can be used to assist people with depression and anxiety disorders. p. 396–397

14.15 Identify the key components of cognitive-behavioural therapy. p. 397

14.16 Identify what the letters in EMDR represent. p. 398

14.17 Explain who EMDR works. p. 398

14.18 Identify for which disorders the following drugs are used: neuroleptic drugs, tricyclics, selective serotonin reuptake inhibitors, monoamine oxidase inhibitors, lithium, and tranquilizers. p. 399–400

14.19 Explain how the following drugs function: neuroleptic drugs, tricyclics, selective serotonin reuptake inhibitors, lithium, and tranquilizers. p. 399–400

14.20 Explain how electroconvulsive therapy (ECT) is used as a therapy. p. 400–401	
14.21 Define psychosurgery and the disorders it is used to treat. p. 401–402	
14.22 Compare the strengths and weaknesses for each therapy. p. 402	
14.23 Compare the training and skills that psychologists and psychiatrists offer for clients. p. 403	
14.24 Understand how culture and gender can impact on the effectiveness of therapy. p. 404	

Practice Multiple-Choice Test

After studying the text and completing the Study Guide activities, answer these questions to determine if you need to review any areas before your exam.

1. The treatment of emotional and behavioural disorders with psychological rather than biological methods is known as:
   a. psychotherapy.
   b. psychosurgery.
   c. psychoneuroimmunology.
   d. psychiatry.

2. Psychoanalysts believe that all maladaptive behaviour results from:
   a. an ineffective ego.
   b. unconscious conflicts.
   c. a fixation at an early stage of psychosexual development.
   d. overuse of defence mechanisms.

3. Urging a client to express thoughts and feelings freely and to verbalize whatever comes to mind without editing or censoring is a technique called:
   a. transference.
   b. interpretation.
   c. abreaction.
   d. free association.

4. Jamie feels very angry toward her psychoanalyst, which is very similar to the feelings she had toward her father. This expression of hatred toward the analyst is an example of:
   a. free association.
   b. transference.
   c. resistance.
   d. repression.

5. The central task of person-centred therapy involves:
   a. replacing irrational thoughts with rational ones.
   b. creating a warm, accepting climate so that the client's natural tendency toward growth will be realized.
   c. replacing repression with insight.
   d. applying the principles of operant and classical conditioning in psychotherapy.

6. Person-centred therapy is best described as:
   a. confrontive.
   b. structured.
   c. nondirective.
   d. objective.

7. Which therapeutic approach seeks to help a person deal with basic aspects of life, its meaning, and its worth?
   a. Gestalt therapy
   b. interpersonal therapy
   c. group therapy
   d. existential therapy

8. A major goal of Gestalt therapy is to:
   a. get people in touch with their feelings.
   b. help people develop critical thinking skills.
   c. overcome barriers that block the path to self-actualization.
   d. teach people to use anxiety in constructive ways.

9. Interpersonal therapy, also called IPT, is successful to a larger extent because it is:
   a. focused on a specific goal.
   b. free of behaviour modification techniques.
   c. quite long and thorough.
   d. based on a complete re-education of the individual.

10. ____________ involves an individual acting out his or her problem relationships with other members of the group playing the significant parts.
    a. Interpersonal therapy
    b. Gestalt therapy
    c. Psychodrama
    d. Token economy

11. Behaviour therapists assume that many distressing psychological problems result from faulty:
    a. defence mechanisms
    b. biochemistry.
    c. reasoning.
    d. learning.

12. Operant conditioning is involved with which of the following?
    a. An event causing an inappropriate positive response is paired with electric shock.
    b. An event causing inappropriate fear is paired with relaxation.
    c. A model demonstrates appropriate action toward a previously feared stimulus.
    d. Positive reinforcers are provided to encourage the performance of desired behaviour.

13. A token economy is involved in which of the following?
    a. Upon performing desired behaviours, a patient receives tokens that can be exchanged for various reinforcers.
    b. An event causing inappropriate fear is paired with relaxation.
    c. An event causing an inappropriate positive response is paired with electric shock.
    d. A situation in which the client provides token appropriate behaviours as a disguise for resistance to therapy.

14. Systematic desensitization is used in the treatment of:
    a. schizophrenia.
    b. mood disorders.
    c. phobias.
    d. somatoform disorders.

15. The technique of flooding is used in which of the following?
    a. direct exposure to feared object without relaxation
    b. imagining painful or sickening stimuli associated with undesirable behaviour
    c. deep muscle relaxation and gradual exposure to feared object
    d. imitating a model responding appropriately in the feared situation

16. Jim wants to quit smoking and tries a technique that involves smoking so much that he feels sick to his stomach. This technique is called:
    a. aversion therapy.
    b. operant therapy.
    c. systematic desensitization.
    d. Gestalt therapy.

17. Albert Ellis believes that abnormal behaviour is caused by:
    a. genetic vulnerability.
    b. irrational behaviour patterns.
    c. irrational thought patterns.
    d. traumatic experiences.

18. What does Aaron Beck call the unreasonable but unquestioned ideas that rule a person's life?
    a. distorted concepts
    b. automatic thoughts
    c. tunnel thinking
    d. thinking tyrants

19. Which of the following is NOT a biological therapy?
    a. ECT
    b. drug therapy
    c. cognitive restructuring
    d. psychosurgery

20. Which of the following drug categories relieves a wide range of symptoms, including hallucinations, delusions, and agitation?
    a. antipsychotics
    b. minor tranquillizers
    c. antidepressants
    d. lithium

21. A patient whose major symptom is a disturbance of mood would probably be prescribed:
    a. antidepressants.
    b. antipsychotics.
    c. major tranquillizers.
    d. antianxiety drugs.

22. ____________ is a type of couples therapy that emphasizes both behaviour change and mutual acceptance.
   a. Integrated behavioural couples therapy (IBCT)
   b. Psychodrama
   c. Encounter group
   d. Traditional cognitive family therapy (TCFT)

23. ____________ is a behavioural technique, used to decrease the frequency of undesirable behaviour; involves withdrawing an individual from all reinforcement for a period of time.
   a. Token economy
   b. Psychodrama
   c. Stimulus satiation
   d. Time out

24. ____________ is a behavioural therapy that exposes obsessive-compulsive disorder patients to objects or situations generating increasing anxiety; patients must agree not to carry out their normal rituals for a specified period of time after exposure.
   a. Flooding
   b. Aversion therapy
   c. Exposure and response prevention
   d. Tornado

Answers to Multiple-Choice Questions

Question Number	Answer	Explanation for application questions
1.	a.	
2.	b.	
3.	d.	
4.	b.	
5.	b.	
6.	c.	
7.	d.	
8.	a.	
9.	a.	
10.	c.	
11.	d.	
12.	d.	
13.	a.	
14.	c.	
15.	a.	
16.	a.	
17.	c.	
18.	b.	
19.	c.	
20.	a.	
21.	a.	
22.	a.	
23.	d.	
24.	a.	

Glossary for Text Language Enhancement

Students identified the following words from the text as needing more explanation. This page can be cut out, folded in half, and used as a bookmark for this chapter.

term	definition
voyeur	pleasure is gained from knowing that those who you watch do not know you are watching them
portability	able to move it around easily
anonymity	nameless
spilling your heart	telling what is very important to you
trivial	of little importance
balks	resists
stark	dramatic
facade	pretence; a false front
badgers	to torment
desensitization	to make less sensitive
hierarchy	step-by-step process
impotence	man not being able to have sex
frigidity	woman not being interested in sex
syllabus	course outline
rituals	repeating a certain behaviour
nausea	uneasy stomach
retch	start to vomit
abstinence	not drinking any alcohol
scenario	situation
stunned	shocked, upset
dragged on	went slowly
confrontational	challenging
relapse	get symptoms again
catastrophic	horrible
delusions	false beliefs
hallucinations	sensations that are imaginary
fidgeting	moving around too much
shuffling gait	walking in small steps
mania	excited state
advocates	people in favour of
deteriorated	became worse
apathy	not caring about anything
irreversible	cannot go back to the original state

Thinking Critically

Evaluation

In your opinion, what are the major strengths and weaknesses of the following approaches to therapy: insight therapy, behaviour therapy, cognitive therapy, and drug therapy?

Point/Counterpoint

From what you have learned in this chapter, prepare a strong argument to support each of these positions:

a. Psychotherapy is generally superior to drug therapy in the treatment of psychological disorders.

b. Drug therapy is generally superior to psychotherapy in the treatment of psychological disorders.

Psychology in Your Life

What questions would you ask a therapist before beginning treatment?